identity
theft

identity
theft

What it is,
How to Prevent it,
and What to do if it
Happens to You

Rob Hamadi

First published in Great Britain in 2004 by Vision Paperbacks,
a division of Satin Publications Ltd.
101 Southwark Street
London SE1 0JF
UK
info@visionpaperbacks.co.uk
www.visionpaperbacks.co.uk
Publisher: Sheena Dewan

ISBN: 1-904132-49-9

2 4 6 8 10 9 7 5 3 1

Cover and text design by ok?design
Printed and bound in the UK by Mackays of Chatham Ltd,
Chatham, Kent

Contents

Acknowledgements

It's not a good idea to speak with people on condition of anonymity and then name them in the acknowledgements, especially when they may work in law enforcement. So to all those people who helped me by giving me the straight scoop: thank you, you know who you are. Thanks also to all the organisations who saved both my time and theirs by ensuring the availability of the fullest possible information online.

A number of agencies provided assistance with the research for this book. In no particular order I'd like to thank Sandra Quinn and Mark Bowerman at APACS; Neil Munroe at Equifax; Megan L Gaffney and others at the United States Department of Justice; far too many records officers at state and federal courts throughout the USA to name – all of whom went the extra mile to answer my supplementary questions; the Royal Mail and the United States Postal Inspection Service; the press officers at the UK's National Criminal Intelligence Service, the Metropolitan Police,

Lloyds TSB, the Home Office, the Department for Work and Pensions, the US Social Security Administration; and London Borough of Brent Registrar Mark Rimmer.

Thanks and appreciation go to all the non-profit organisations and individuals who set out to help ordinary people with the problem of identity theft, especially the Privacy Rights Clearinghouse and the Identity Theft Resource Center, Ross Anderson and Mike Bond at the University of Cambridge and the Electronic Privacy Information Center.

Thanks also to all the members of www.flyertalk.com for the invaluable tips and advice that made the travelling part of the research less of a chore.

Thanks, of course, to my publisher Sheena Dewan for giving me the opportunity to write this book and to my editor Charlotte Cole for nurse-maiding a first time author.

Finally, extra special thanks to Jen Schwartzman and Betsy Broder at the Federal Trade Commission for all their help and to the FTC itself for leading the world in the fight against identity theft.

Introduction

♂ The wrong Mr Bond

In February 2003, 72-year-old retired charity worker Derek Bond, from Bristol, England arrived in South Africa for a wine-tasting holiday with his wife Audrey. Within hours he was arrested at gunpoint and thrown into a Durban jail. Twenty days later Mr Bond, who was innocent of any crime, was finally released.

The FBI was hunting a fugitive by the name of Derek Sykes, wanted in connection with a multi-million dollar tele marketing fraud. Unfortunately for Mr Bond, one identity wasn't enough for Sykes. Back in 1989 he started using the name Derek Bond, along with Mr Bond's date of birth and passport number.

Following an anonymous tip-off, Sykes was eventually arrested in Las Vegas, Nevada where he was living under the name of Robert James Grant. He pleaded guilty to money-laundering conspiracy in October 2003 and was sentenced to over five years without parole in June 2004. None of this was much comfort to Mr Bond.

No matter where in the world you live, the chances are that you, or someone you know, has been a victim of identity theft. Frank Abagnale, once arguably the world's greatest fraudster and now a leading security expert, has called identity theft 'the crime of this century'. In 2003 the United States Federal Trade Commission received over half a million – 516,740 – fraud and identity theft complaints, up by a quarter from 2002's figure of 404,000. In the same year UK anti-fraud operation Credit Industry Fraud Avoidance System (CIFAS) logged 101,000 cases, up from 74,000 in the previous year.

So what is identity theft? This broad term covers a range of crimes, from simple credit card fraud, through taking out loans or applying for work in another person's name, to the wholesale cooption of an individual's entire life. All the crimes have two things in common – the criminal has had access to and exploited our personal details. In order to succeed the criminal must also have more knowledge than the victim about how the systems concerned function and their inherent vulnerabilities.

In this book I set out to give you the reader access to the same information and methods used by the criminals. This knowledge has been distilled from interviews with and research on people who understand identity theft in intimate detail, from the criminals themselves to the law enforcement officers whose job it is to catch them. By using the information in this book you will learn the various ways your identity is recorded and the many ways it can be stolen, and you will therefore be able to minimise your exposure to identity theft. However there is no such thing as zero risk in the real world. No matter how many precautions we take the law of averages means that we may still, eventually, fall victim to one of these crimes. The final chapter in this book takes you through some practical steps to try to put things right.

While the case studies and legal notes in this book refer mainly to the UK and US due to lack of space, the principles are general and much of the material is relevant to elsewhere. Residents of Canada, Australia and New Zealand can find useful contacts at the back. Not all identity theft is as extreme as that of Mr Bond's. Much is financial, the following being characteristic:

🔒 A classic case of identity theft

In April 2002 Edward Smith, a former resident of Orlando, Florida was convicted of identity theft and sentenced to four-and-a-half years in prison by a Florida court.

Smith harvested personal information belonging to his victims from a legitimate online database and used it to apply for credit cards and loans in their names. At his indictment the court heard that he had made more than $35,000 worth of fraudulent purchases, including a Harley Davidson motorcycle.

Florida Department of Law Enforcement Special Agent Robert Ivey told the court, 'This was a classic identity theft operation in which Smith falsely obtained credit at stores throughout east-central Florida, and the manner in which he obtained the personal information made anyone in the state, and even the country, a potential victim.'

While Smith's case is as typical as Mr Bond's is tragic, both eventually came to an end. Perhaps the worst thing that identity theft victims have to deal with is when the crime repeatedly comes back to haunt them. Take the case of Malcolm Byrd – it really is best to minimise the risks of having your identity stolen in the first place.

The victim gets arrested again!

Item I 9 on the agenda for the June 2003 meeting of the Kenosha County, Wisconsin, Board of Supervisors read 'Claims: Malcolm Byrd – wrongfully arrested'. Okay, so wrongful arrest is a terrible thing, but these things happen, don't they? In Mr Byrd's case the answer is yes – every few months!

Malcolm's problems began in 1998 when a man arrested for drug dealing gave his name as Malcolm Byrd. Since then the real Malcolm Byrd has been repeatedly arrested, lost his job, been refused unemployment benefit and had his drivers licence suspended. In an attempt to resolve matters he even visited the District Attorney and was provided with court documents proving his innocence – only to be arrested again on charges filed after his declaration of innocence was issued.

The problem is that when a criminal is arrested and gives a stolen ID police rarely check too deeply into it. The crook is then bailed and, when he fails to turn up in court, an arrest warrant is issued in the identity theft victim's name. It gets worse, even when the victim proves he is not the crook his name stays on the criminal's file as a known alias and can be nearly impossible to get rid of.

A note on case studies

Except in a very few cases, all victim names in this book are fictitious. It's my belief that these people have suffered enough. The exceptions are cases that were well publicised in the news media, such as that of Mr Bond, in which case the victims and their names are common knowledge. By the same token, where they have been reported most of the criminals are given their real names in the case studies. Of course, in any example where a prosecution is ongoing the allegations are only allegations and the defendant(s) must be regarded as innocent until proven guilty. Finally, while all of the victims' stories are based on fact, some are constructed by combining two or more cases, in order to better illustrate a point.

Chapter 1
What is Identity?

Three hundred years ago most people rarely left their home-town. Indeed whole generations were born, lived and died in the same house or street as the previous generation. Identity then was a simple concept – we were all known, personally, to everybody we were likely to meet. Today, populations have become more mobile, and increased prosperity has given the average person access to modern financial instruments, such as credit cards and bank accounts. As a result there is now a clear need for an objective means for an individual to prove his or her identity to others. Because this need did not appear overnight, but rather evolved over time, institutions ranging from banks to bars have adopted ad hoc approaches to the problem of verifying identity, usually involving the use of already-existing documents. The fundamental security problem with this kind of 'function creep' is that many of the documents used to prove identity were never designed to do so. For example, utilities bills (gas, electricity, water, etc) are intended to tell you how much you must pay your supplier, not to prove who you are or where you live. Even the passport was not designed to prove your identity, but rather as a 'token' to show that you had your ruler's permission to cross national borders.

In this chapter I will examine the most common tokens and identifiers, looking at the ways in which they are used and highlighting the methods whereby criminals can exploit their inherent vulnerabilities. First though, let's look at a documented example of the extreme consequences of the inadequacies in our system of identity.

♪ Mistaken Identity – Michelle's story

In July 2000 the US Senate Judiciary Committee's Subcommittee on Technology, Terrorism and Government Information held a hearing on identity theft. One of the witnesses was a 29-year-old international banker from Los Angeles named Michelle Brown. Her story is frightening.

In January 1998 Michelle filed an application to rent a property. Shortly afterwards an identity thief named Heddi Larae Ille stole the rental application, containing Michelle's personal information, from the landlord's property management office. Michelle told the Senate subcommittee:

'It was a scenario I had only previously known through unbelievable stories painted in Hollywood: someone becomes you, erases your life, and through their destructive behaviours, complicates your own existence to an extreme level where you no longer know how to just live day after day. Your life becomes the life consumed by unravelling the unthinkable acts that your perpetrator has done in your perceived skin.

What is Identity?

'I discovered on January 12, 1999, the existence of this shadow identity that I have been anxiously trying to expel from my life ever since. To be truthful, I don't think I will ever be able to close the books entirely on this menace's activities. I dearly wish I could, but what I know now translates to the fact that I will always be dealing with this alter reality I am plagued with.

'Over the course of a year and a half, my name, personal identifiers and records were grossly misused to obtain over $50,000 in goods and services, to rent properties, and to engage in federal criminal activities – namely drug trafficking. During the course of 1999, I spent countless sleepless nights and seemingly endless days, dedicating my valuable time, energy, peace of mind, and what should have been a normal life, trying to restore my credit and my life.'

Sadly, the perpetrator's financial fraud was not the worst of it. In May 1999, Heddi Larae Ille was arrested in Texas for smuggling 3,000 pounds of marijuana. She identified herself as Michelle Brown to the Drug Enforcement Agency and a federal magistrate. We can only assume she was released on some kind of bail, because the next month a federal felony warrant was issued for her arrest, again in Michelle's name. Ille was eventually re-arrested in July, but Michelle's problems were about to get worse:

'In September 1999, returning from a trip to Cabo San Lucas [in Mexico], I was held at LAX's [Los Angeles International Airport] Customs and Immigration for an hour while I explained the circumstances of my erroneous link with her criminal record (after my passport was swiped in the computer). As I presented endless documentation of court records, police filings, etc, and explained my situation in a stream of tears, I knew then that I had become erroneously linked with Heddi's criminal record. The agents questioned my story and documentation, and treated me very suspiciously – like I was the criminal. After the Police Detective [who had been investigating Michelle's identity theft case] was called and vouched for me, I was allowed to leave. I feared being arrested or being taken into custody. I found out later that, even though Heddi had already been in police custody at a jail since July, the DEA posted a lookout for "me" in the system. They neglected to let me know that I might want to be prepared for this type of confusion at any time.'

Ille was eventually convicted of three felony counts (perjury, grand theft and possession of stolen property) and sentenced to three concurrent two-year jail sentences. The following year she was also sentenced to 73 months for the drugs charges. For Michelle however, the nightmare went on.

'I filed various statements and affidavits, had documents notarised, made thousands of phone calls to creditors, governmental authorities, etc, and continually set in motion the next level of protection for further follow up and monitoring. I alerted all the proper authorities, filed all the right papers, made the right phone calls, and diligently remained actively adamant to restore my perfect credit and my good name. I would estimate that the time lost toward clearing my credit, attempting to clear my criminal record, and to sever myself free from this menacing being, amounted to somewhere in excess of 500 hours of my time. At the time, the burden seemed like it cost me a lifetime.

'For me, the most personally frightening moment was dealing with LAX's Customs and fearing an erroneous arrest. Because of this situation, I purposely have NOT gone out of the country for fear of some mishap, confusion, language barrier, that may land me in prison for some unknown period of time. I do not deserve to be in this predicament and do not deserve to feel imprisoned by the US borders. I still fear what might happen as I cross the US border and I cannot get assurance from any governmental agency that this situation will never happen again.'

Michelle's story, while dramatic, is far from unique. Although identity theft is often primarily financial crime, the fact is that criminals who are prepared to commit one type of crime will usually commit others. When held to account for one crime, identity thieves generally have little hesitation in identifying themselves as one of their other victims.

The three elements of identity

A report for the UK government's Cabinet Office in 2002 defines the three basic elements of identity as biometric identity, attributed identity and biographical identity. It goes on to expand upon these three types of identity:

- **Biometric Identity:** attributes that are unique to an individual, ie fingerprints, voice, retina, facial structure, DNA profile, hand geometry, heat radiation, etc;
- **Attributed identity:** the components of a person's identity that are given at birth, including their full name, date and place of birth, parents' names and addresses;
- **Biographical identity:** identity which builds up over time. This covers life events and how a person interacts with structured society, including:

- ♣ Registration of birth;
- ♣ Details of education/qualifications;
- ♣ Electoral register entries;
- ♣ Details of benefits claimed/taxes paid;
- ♣ Employment history;
- ♣ Registration of marriage;
- ♣ Mortgage account information/property ownership;
- ♣ Insurance policies;
- ♣ History of interaction with organisations such as banks, creditors, utilities, public authorities.

Tokens and identifiers

In this context, an identifier is a characteristic (your appearance, fingerprint, full name, Social Security number, etc) that, either by itself or in combination with other data, more or less uniquely identifies a person. A token is a physical or electronic object that may be given or shown as a demonstration of a fact or event (eg a bus ticket may be shown to an inspector to demonstrate that you have paid your bus fare, while a birth certificate is an official record of a historical event). Today many tokens are used as identifiers. Here are some of the most common identifiers, and the tokens that represent them:

Biometric identifiers

Although biometric identifiers such as finger prints and retinal scans are very much the technology of the moment, and are being talked about in the context of 'biometric passports' and ID cards, the truth is that biometric identification is not new. When the villagers three hundred years ago recognised each other by sight, they were using a basic form of biometric identification. Whenever we recognise somebody's voice on the telephone we are using a type of biometric ID. Even our signature could be termed a biometric identifier. It is when we come to create tokens such as ID cards and database records to record biometric identifiers for the purposes of comparison and identification that biometric identity becomes vulnerable to attack.

A cautionary note on biometrics

A great deal of government activity on both sides of the Atlantic right now focuses on biometric identification. Some commentators appear to believe that such technology will be a universal solution to issues of identity. In fact, biometric authentication is far from foolproof. In all there are many types of attack, ranging from an insider compromising the database, which stores the biometric characteristics, to an outsider fooling the sensor. Here I shall look briefly at the latter, specifically fingerprint scanners.

There are a number of types of fingerprint scanner. Two of the most common types are capacitive scanners, which measure minute electrical differences caused by the difference in distance between the peaks and troughs of the skin on the finger and the sensor, and optical scanners, which take a 'picture' of the fingerprint.

Capacitive scanners

Researchers in Germany and elsewhere have identified three ways of fooling capacitive fingerprint scanners. All these methods rely on the fact that each time somebody uses the scanner they leave tiny traces of grease behind, transferred from the skin. These grease traces, made up of the skin's natural oils, form an image of the fingerprint. The three techniques are:

- 🔒 Breathe on the scanner. Some of the most basic types of capacitive scanner can be fooled simply by cupping your hands over the scanning plate and breathing gently.
- 🔒 The bag of water. Researchers also report achieving success by placing a thin-walled bag of cold water onto the sensor plate. An unlubricated condom would appear to be ideal.
- 🔒 Graphite powder. The most reliable technique involves dusting the fingerprint on the sensor plate with graphite powder, such as that found in a child's fingerprint kit. A piece of adhesive film is then stretched over the plate's surface and gentle pressure is applied.

Optical scanners

Some of the first and best work in this area was carried out by Japanese mathematician Tsutomu Matsumoto, at the Graduate School of Environment and Information Sciences at the University of Yokohama. Involving the creation of a false finger, it draws heavily on traditional forensics.

The starting point is a fingerprint on a piece of glass or similar material. If the fingerprint is of poor quality it can be enhanced by dusting with graphite powder (the child's fingerprint kit again) or by holding it above a small pot of cyanoacrylate adhesive (such as Superglue), which sticks to the moisture in the print – a forensic technique used by police forces worldwide.

The print is then photographed, scanned into a computer, made into an inverted image and sharpened in an image-editing programme. The next step is to make a mould. Many electronics hobby shops around the world sell photo-sensitive copper-clad boards (along with instructions) for the legitimate purpose of making electronic printed circuit boards. Matsumoto and others have demonstrated that by etching the print onto the board it is possible to create a mould.

The final step is to create the finger. Various studies recommend using a one-to-one mix of gelatine and water, repeatedly microwaving the mix to remove bubbles and using high-quality gelatine to retain moisture. In any case the gelatine is poured onto the mould producing, when set, a prosthetic layer that can be attached to a real finger.

Matsumoto reported an 80 per cent success rate with this technique. As one anonymous security writer comments: 'Once inside the restricted area, eat the gummy finger and proceed.'

Are other forms of biometric ID any better?

Researchers report having successfully fooled many other systems, including facial recognition and iris scanning. A websearch on the word 'fool' and 'biometric', 'fingerprint' or 'iris scan' turns up many such examples.

The final word should go to security expert Bruce Schnier. Commenting on Matsumoto's work he said 'Matsumoto is not a professional fake-finger scientist; he's a mathematician. He didn't use expensive equipment or a specialised laboratory. He used $10 of ingredients you could buy, and whipped up his gummy fingers in the equivalent of a home kitchen. If he could do this, then any semi-professional can almost certainly do much much more.'

Attributed identifiers

The simplest attributed identifier is our full name. Another is our National Insurance or Social Security number. These identifiers are represented on various tokens, usually government-issued documents that underpin our 'official' identity. These documents, which include our birth certificate, passport, etc, are often called 'breeder documents' because they can be used to generate other so-called proofs of identity.

The most widely abused attributed identifiers or tokens thereof are the birth certificate and, in the US, the Social Security number.

Birth certificates

Under English law parents have six weeks from the birth of a child to register the birth with their local Registrar of Births, Deaths and Marriages. The parents must provide the following information:

Child
- Date and place of birth; if the birth is one of twins, triplets, etc; the time of each child's birth will also be needed;
- Sex of the child;
- The forename(s) and surname in which it is intended that the child will be brought up.

Father (if his details are to be entered in the register)

- Forename(s) and surname;
- Date and place of birth;
- Occupation at the time of the child's birth or, if not employed at that time, the last occupation.

Mother
- Forename(s) and surname;
- Maiden surname if the mother is, or has been, married;
- Date and place of birth;
- Occupation at the time of the child's birth or, if not employed at that time, the last occupation;
- Usual address at the date of the birth;
- Date of marriage, if married to the child's father at the time of the birth;
- Number of previous children by the present husband and by any former husband.

Once registered, the birth record is a public document. Anybody is entitled to obtain a certified copy of any UK birth certificate whatsoever for a minimal fee. For England and Wales, this can be done by turning up at the registry office where the birth was registered or at the Family Records Centre in London. Copies can also be ordered by post, telephone, fax and even over the internet. It is a public document, so the registrar cannot demand ID or refuse to supply a certificate. For births registered in Scotland or Northern Ireland, you need to contact the appropriate General Register Office or the local Registration Office.

In the United States matters are somewhat different because vital records (as records of births, deaths, etc are known) are organised on a state-by-state basis. Some states do require ID of some description to obtain a copy of a birth certificate, and some even cross-reference births and deaths. The practice is far from uniform however. In 1999 John M Hotchner, director of the US Office of Passport Policy, told the House Committee on the Judiciary: 'There are many thousands of offices nationwide authorised to issue certified copies of US birth certificates, which come in hundreds of different formats.'

Compounding the problem of the variety of certificates is the ease with which copies can be obtained. Copies of legitimate birth certificates can often be obtained through state, county or municipal authorities – generally upon presentation of nothing more than a driver's license. Many states have unrestricted access to vital records, in some cases allowing the purchase of copies of birth certificates for different individuals.

What can a criminal do with a birth certificate?

♂ 'Ghosting' – new lives for old

In the 1970s author Fredrick Forsysth's bestselling novel *Day of the Jackal* was published. In it the protagonist, an assassin, applies for and receives a British passport by first obtaining the birth certificate of a dead child, who was born at about the same time as himself.

In Forsyth's book the character visited graveyards and looked at the grave markers, a practice sometimes known as 'Tombstoning'. In modern times criminals simply consult newspaper obituaries or public registers. One source has claimed that there was a time when anyone visiting the UK's Public

Records Office could consult the register of deaths and find pencil marks next to certain entries, allegedly signs left by terrorists and other identity thieves, to let their colleagues know that that name was 'taken'.

At the most basic level, the birth certificate contains your mother's maiden name and your date of birth, two pieces of information that are often used by banks and other financial institutions to verify the identity of anybody claiming to be a customer.

A more serious problem, however, is that even though copy birth certificates have the words 'Warning: A certificate is not evidence of identity' printed on them, they are still widely accepted as such. Ultimately the birth certificate is the ultimate breeder document, and can be used to obtain a passport, driving licence, National Insurance or Social Security number, and much more.

To cite one example, the US Department of State's Diplomatic Security Service, which has statutory authority to investigate passport fraud, recently had a case of an alien-trafficking operation that recruited drug-addicted US citizens (out of a methadone clinic) to obtain and sell their birth certificates. The birth certificates were then used illegally for a number of purposes – the primary one being application for a US passport.

Additionally, fraudulent applicants are able to obtain the legitimate birth certificates of deceased persons because the UK and some US states do not cross-reference the records of births and deaths. There have been cases where an individual born in one state is killed in an accident in another. Someone spots the obituary, gets a copy of the birth certificate, obtains identification under the identity, and applies for a passport – all before the death record is filed in either state.

⚷ A real-life 'Jackal'

In April 2004 terrorist James William Kilgore, a member of the Symbionese Liberation Army (SLA), was sentenced to 48 months in federal prison for a 1975 bomb offence. He was also sentenced to a consecutive six months in federal prison for passport fraud connected to multiple fraudulent passports obtained by the defendant using the identity of a deceased child. Kilgore was later sentenced to six years in state prison for the 1975 murder of a bank customer in a bank robbery. This sentence will begin after his federal imprisonment is completed.

Kilgore, age 56, had been a fugitive for 26 years when he was apprehended in South Africa in November 2002. Kilgore, who was originally from Oregon and the San Francisco Bay Area, became a fugitive after the arrest of fellow SLA members including Patty Hearst on 18 September 1975.

Kilgore fled to the Milwaukee, Wisconsin/St Paul, Minnesota areas where he first obtained a false United States passport in the name of Charles William Paper, who was in fact a deceased 10-month-old infant. Kilgore established a life in South Africa under the paper identity, renewing the passport twice, the second time at the US Consulate in South Africa in 1994.

The US Social Security number

The Social Security number, or SSN, is one of the most important identifiers in the US. The 9-digit SSN is comprised of three parts:

1. The first three digits are the area number, indicating either the state in which the SSN was issued (if issued before 1972) or the state given in the mailing address on the application form after that year.
2. The second two digits are the group number. These are issued in the order odd 01 to 09, even 10 to 98, even 02 to 08 and finally odd 11 to 99.
3. The final four digits are the serial number. These at least are issued consecutively, 0001 to 9999.

In the US the Social Security Administration advises parents to apply for a Social Security number for their child at the same time as they give information for the child's birth certificate. The state's vital statistics office will send the Social Security Administration the information needed. Parents who apply later must show at least two documents as evidence of the child's age, identity and citizenship; and show evidence of their own identity. Documents the SSA may accept as evidence of age, identity and citizenship for a baby or older child are:

Age
- Birth certificate (preferred);
- Religious record of birth recorded before three months of age (eg baptismal record).

Identity
- Doctor, clinic, hospital record;
- Religious record;
- Daycare centre/school record;
- Adoption record;
- School ID card.

Citizenship
- Birth certificate;
- Other document showing US place of birth;

Some documents the SSA may accept as proof of identity for the parent are:
- Driver's license;
- Employer ID card
- Passport;
- Marriage or divorce record;
- Health insurance card (not a Medicare card);
- Military record;
- Life insurance policy;
- School ID card.

From June 2002, the Social Security Administration began contacting the office that issued the birth record to make sure that the record is valid.

It is still possible for an adult to obtain an SSN. People who apply for a new Social Security number must furnish at least two documents to establish age, identity and US citizenship or lawful non-citizen status. However an in-person interview must be conducted if the applicant is age 12 or older and is applying for an original SSN. In addition, US-born applicants age 12 or older must explain why they do not already have a Social Security number.

In the US a SSN is used for virtually everything that matters. Although originally only intended for social security purposes, in 1961 the Internal Revenue Service began using Social Security numbers as taxpayer identification numbers. This meant it was required on any records the IRS was interested in such as payroll, banking, stock market, property, and other financial transactions. From there it was only a short step to the SSN becoming a universal ID number, used for medical records, insurance, education and even credit cards. Even state departments of motor vehicles started using it as a driver number, although considerable effort has been expended to change this.

What use is an SSN to a criminal?

To all intents and purposes, in most computer systems, you are your Social Security number. Once the criminal has it he can become you for the purposes of obtaining credit cards, loans and even a driver's licence. Because the SSN is used so widely it is very easy to steal, and the SSA's extra security measures make existing SSNs all the more valuable. Many of the Social Security numbers used by the 9/11 terrorists were stolen. It is, of course, an offence to:

🔒 Use someone else's Social Security number unlawfully;
🔒 Give false information when applying for a number; or
🔒 Alter, buy or sell Social Security cards.

But naturally, the thing about criminals is that they have little or no respect for the law, as well-known actor Will Smith found out.

☙ The dark side of celebrity impersonation

Actor Will Smith had no idea that his identity had been stolen, until he attempted to buy a new home and found his credit had been compromised.

42-year-old Pennsylvania man Carlos Lomax had got hold of Mr Smith's Social Security number and used it, together with the actor's full name, Willard C Smith, to open 14 credit accounts in his victim's name, running up debts of $33,000.

US Postal Inspectors and the Financial Crimes Task Force of Southwestern Pennsylvania arrested Lomax for identity theft and, in December 2002, Lomax was sentenced to serve 37 months in jail and pay $64,000 in restitution.

☙ Accidental identity thieves

Not all misuse of an SSN is malicious. The US Social Security Administration like to tell the story of the Social Security number 'issued by Woolworth'. In 1938 wallet manufacturer the EH Ferree company in Lockport, New York decided to promote its product by inserting a sample Social Security card into each wallet to show how a card would fit. Company Vice President and Treasurer Douglas Patterson came up with the idea of using the actual SSN of his secretary, Mrs Hilda Schrader Whitcher, which was 078-05-1120.

The wallet was sold by Woolworth stores and other department stores all over the US. Even though the card was only half the size of a real card, was printed all in red, and had the word 'specimen' written across the face, many purchasers of the wallet adopted the SSN as their own. In the peak year of 1943, 5,755 people were using Hilda's number.

The SSA responded by cancelling the number (giving Mrs Whitcher a new one) and publicising that it was wrong to use it. However, the number continued to be used for many years. In all, over 40,000 people reported this as their SSN. As late as 1977, 12 people were found to still be using the SSN 'issued by Woolworth'.

Although Mrs Whitcher saw the funny side of the mistake, it was mostly a nuisance. The FBI even showed up at her door to ask her about the widespread use of her number. In later years she observed: 'They started using the number. They thought it was their own. I can't understand how people can be so stupid. I can't understand that.'

The UK National Insurance number

The UK National Insurance number is similar in some ways to the US SSN. It is an attributed identifier in that it is issued by the government, it is used for social security benefits and taxation purposes and, in theory, every number is unique. In practice however the NI number is very different from an SSN.

NI numbers are issued automatically to children in the UK, for whom child benefit has been paid, shortly before their sixteenth birthday. It is nine characters long and consists of letters and numbers in the form XY123456Z.

However the UK NI number is nowhere near as pervasive in private life as the US SSN. Whereas US credit reports are indexed by SSN the NI number is nowhere to be found on a UK credit report. And while US banks require an SSN to open an account or sign up for a credit card, it's possible to get a credit card from a UK bank in ten minutes without ever divulging your NI number.

Whereas the US SSN is truly a unique identifier, there is no such commercial sector confidence in the UK NI number. There are, in fact, many more NI numbers in circulation in the UK than there are people. In a debate in the House of Commons in March 2001 Conservative MP David Willetts observed that 'Britain now has 81 million national insurance numbers for 60 million people ... there are 25 million more numbers than there are people in the United Kingdom.' Furthermore UK and European data protection law is much stricter than that in the US. A source at one of the UK's major credit reference agencies identifies three obstacles to indexing credit reports by NI number:

1. Coverage – not everybody has one;
2. Data protection – credit rating agencies would need special consent to use the NI number for that purpose;
3. NI numbers are not regarded as 'strong enough' for the purpose.

What use is an NI number to a criminal?

Given that NI numbers are used for taxation and benefits there are two obvious reasons to steal a person's national insurance number – tax fraud and benefit fraud. Recent trends suggest that cases of pure benefit fraud involving fraudulent use on NI numbers tend to be small-scale independent criminals, often hijacking the identity of somebody they know. The third, less obvious reason to steal an NI number is illegal immigration; this is the most common type of NI number fraud observed by the UK's Department of Work and Pensions. Sources suggest that in these cases NI numbers are traded by organised criminals as part of a package of identity documents rather than being sold on their own.

🔓 A benefit fraud example

A criminal who wants to claim benefits while working must lie in order to do so. In particular he wants to avoid anyone connecting his employment with the fact that he is claiming benefits. But both the employer and the benefits agency will need his NI number – and if the NI numbers match he could be found out. The solution? Steal somebody else's.

A fraud investigator at a Scottish council received a call from a colleague in the Inland Revenue. It seemed that someone was paying double Income Tax and National Insurance contributions. The industrious individual appeared to be holding down two jobs at the same time, hundreds of miles apart.

The investigator formally contacted the local employer and asked them to provide details of the person the National Insurance number related to. These were eventually supplied and they revealed that there were two people using the same NI number, the person to whom it had been issued and another man, working locally.

Upon looking into the name and address provided by the local employer the investigator discovered that over £150 a week Income Support, £39 a week Housing Benefit and £11 a week Council Tax Benefit was being paid at the address and to the individual named by the employer. All these payments were based on the person's true NI number and the declared fact he was unemployed.

Further checks established that the (by this time) suspect had been employed at the company for over three years and had been receiving benefits throughout the whole period. A quick calculation revealed that throughout the period the person was working, he had claimed a total of over £30,000 in benefits.

The suspect was charged with fraud and prosecuted. In addition to being prosecuted, he was also required to reimburse the council and the DSS the whole of the £31,000 he had falsely claimed.

Similarly illegal immigrants who want to work in the UK need a National Insurance number to give to their employers. In May 2002, the *Sunday Mirror* sent an undercover reporter to seek work on a construction site, posing as an illegal immigrant. According to the paper, the reporter was approached within minutes and offered a National Insurance number for £850.

Biographical identifiers

There is a number of aspects of our biographical identity, particularly in the financial arena, that is of great interest to identity thieves. Following the passage of new money-laundering regulations in the UK, banks are required to verify the name and address of their customers before opening an account. They accomplish this by requiring two identifiers, one showing the person's name and another their address. The following list is compiled from the proofs of name or address required by several UK banks:

- Driving licence;
- Photo student identification/matriculation card (from a recognised university or college);
- Inland Revenue tax notifications (P60, P45, Notice of Coding);
- Benefit Agency letter;
- Personal bank account cheque to open the account;
- Works identity card (only acceptable at branches);
- Cheque guarantee/ATM/debit/credit card (only acceptable at branches);
- Utility bill (within last six months);
- Bank, credit union, building society or credit card statement;
- Recent mortgage statement (within last 12 months);
- Rent card or tenancy agreement;
- Home insurance certificate or policy/motor insurance certificate or policy;
- TV licence renewal notification;
- University/college letter of acceptance/enrolment/offer;
- Local Authority tax/rates bill;
- Letter from employer or contract of employment;
- Payslips.

The evidence of 'function creep' is clear. Many of the above documents were never intended a proof of identity or address, yet they are being used as such. Further weaknesses in the system are that many types of document, such as driving licenses, tax papers, bank statements and benefits documents, can be listed as proof of name by one bank and proof of address by another. Identity thieves exploit this lack of standards by creating chains of documentation and shuffling documents between organisations. Eventually they can breed a solid financial identity from the flimsiest of starter material.

Driving licences

One of the most useful forms of biographical identity is the driving licence. In the United States it has become a de facto identification card while in the UK it is accepted as proof of identity for everything from bank accounts to state benefits to credit cards.

The UK's Driver and Vehicle Licensing Agency (DVLA) lists the following documentation as acceptable confirmation of your identity:

- Full valid current passport;
- Birth certificate;
- Certificate of registry of birth (provided your name is present on the certificate);
- Adoption certificate;
- ID Card issued by a member state of the EC/EEA;
- Travel Documents issued by the Home Office;
- Certificate of naturalisation or registration.

They go on to say 'Note – Birth certificates are not absolute proof of identity and so we may ask you to provide other evidence to allow us to check your identity'. In practice this means that the applicant's photograph must be signed by somebody else who will corroborate that they are who they say they are. The DVLA can only check a proportion of these counter-signatories, and even when they do they can not be as rigorous as they might like, as BBC reporter Paul Kenyon found out.

🔓 Reporter steals Home Secretary's ID

In 2002 BBC investigative reporter Paul Kenyon went to the UK's Family Records Centre in London and asked for a copy of the birth certificate for one David Blunkett, the UK's Home Secretary, who has responsibility for the police and the security services. In short order he had a driving licence in Mr Blunkett's name (but with Kenyon's photograph).

'It's got his personal details on it but my photo.' Mr Kenyon said, explaining that he now had enough ID to get credit in Mr Blunkett's name and potentially wreak havoc in his private financial life.

There are many more examples. Simply typing 'birth certificate' 'passport' 'dead child' into an internet search engine turns up dozens of results, many of them instruction manuals on how to commit the crime. I am even aware of cases where people have obtained copies of prosecution and conviction histories from the UK's Police National Computer using only a copy birth certificate and a credit card bill as evidence of identity. This is despite the fact that such information is regarded as among the most sensitive personal data held by any public authority in the UK.

ᕹ Marriage and the bogus utility bill

The concept of using a false identity as a means of gaining residence in a country by marriage is nothing new. But one registrar of marriages in London has observed a trend.

'If someone wants to get married we ask for evidence of identity and nationality (usually a passport) plus proof of address,' the registrar said. 'The requirement for evidence of address is an extra hurdle, and that created a market for fraudulent documentation'.

Over a period of time the registrar noticed that many of the utility bills and bank statements being presented had something in common. Although each would show a unique name and address, the transaction history or bill total would be identical to those on documents presented by other couples – down to the last detail.

Another warning sign is utility bills apparently for an address in one town being stamped as paid on the other side of the country.

The trade in bogus utility bills, if we accept it as such, is probably driven by organised crime. But the consequences can be devastating even for those of us who wouldn't know how to find an organised criminal if we tried.

'We've even had cases of people turning up to get married and finding that an identity thief has already got married using their identity – at the same office!' the registrar explained.

There are many other examples of biographic identifiers in use today. These include our email addresses, usernames and passwords for online services, ATM or cash machine cards and Personal Identification Numbers (PINs).

Chapter 2

How to steal an Identity

Who steals an Identity

Both small-time fraudsters and organised criminal business trade in identifiers. A 2003 report by the UK's National Criminal Intelligence Service concluded it can be said with a reasonable degree of certainty that:

- Identity fraud cuts across most criminal sectors: illegal immigration, drugs trafficking, money laundering, vehicle theft and frauds against the public and private sector.
- The primary purpose of false identities is to enable serious and organised criminals to conceal themselves, their activities and their assets.
- They may also facilitate specific criminal acts, such as people smuggling or benefit fraud. In addition, false identities are sold for money.
- A false identity document can be obtained by counterfeiting or forgery, fraudulent application or misuse of

someone else's document. Theft and corruption can play a supporting role. Some serious and organised criminals undertake these activities themselves; others turn to their contacts or to specialist providers to meet their needs.

♂ The forgery factory

Many of the specialist providers of ID operate on a large scale. In early 2002 Bais Sulaiman, 45 and his wife Warula Sulaiman, 28 appeared at Southwark Crown Court and pleaded guilty to charges of production of forged documentation. Bais also admitted possession of 13,000 blank identity documents.

Metropolitan police SCD6 Economic and Specialist Crime OCU Detectives raided a home in South London and found what can only be described as an 'identity factory'. From the address police seized computing and card manufacturing equipment, plastic card printer and embosser, card readers and a top-of-the-range industrial colour laser printer, along with four computer systems, laminators and scanners.

From elsewhere in the property, items seized included bank stamps, Immigration and Home Office stamps, and Nigerian visa and passport renewal stamps. Three garages were also found to contain filing cabinets full of National Insurance cards (blank) and various other forged blank documents. Police investigations showed that in excess of 2,600 identities had been 'produced'.

Types of identity theft

There are three distinct categories of identity theft. They are account takeover, application fraud and the wholesale assumption of identity.

Account takeover

Also known as account hijacking, this is one of the most common types of identity theft. The simplest form of account takeover is where a criminal finds a credit card receipt with the card number, expiry date and name of their victim. They will then use that information to make purchases by post, telephone or online – so-called Card Not Present fraud. The next level of refinement involves credit card cloning. The thief makes a copy of their victim's card and uses it as if it were their own. At the furthest extreme criminals will put together enough information about their victim so as to be able to successfully impersonate them to their bank and other organisations. They then call the bank to order a replacement card or register a change of address, thus completely taking over the account. The account takeover technique is also used online, with everything from email accounts to bank accounts.

☞ Card Not Present thieves end up doing time

A typical example of the simplest form of account hijacking is provided by the case of David Sacrista-Longares and Jordi Rams I Delas, two Spaniards working as head waiters in London.

One of New Scotland Yard's specialist fraud units was contacted by the manager of a duty-free jewellers in the Dutch Antilles, who reported that he and other businesses had been the victims of mail order frauds through which expensive watches had been delivered to various addresses in London. The merchants were never paid of course because, although the watches were 'paid for' by credit card, the people ordering the goods were not the real owners of the cards.

When the next suspicious order was placed, with delivery requested by Federal Express, police were waiting at the delivery address and arrested Longares when he collected the package, at which time he produced false identification papers.

The 'black' American Express card used in the transaction had been legitimately used at The Bluebird Club in Chelsea, where Delas was employed as head waiter and where he obtained the card details. It transpired that both Longares and Delas shared a bedsit at the address given for the delivery of the package.

At court, Longares and Delas pleaded guilty to conspiracy to defraud, and were sentenced to 18 months' imprisonment and 12 months' imprisonment respectively.

Of course not all case are that straightforward.

🔌 Sometimes the crook is never caught

New Yorker Brian called his bank to ask where his monthly statement was. He was told it was in the mail. When after another week it still hadn't arrived, he wasn't too worried: It's probably got lost, he thought, I'll get another one in a few months.

It was only when a couple of weeks later he called the bank to find out his balance that he got a shock. 'In fact, your account has not been in credit since you moved to California,' the call centre worker remarked, after telling him he was overdrawn.

Six weeks prior to this call an identity thief had written to Brian's bank, giving his account number and Social Security number and advising them he had moved to California's Bay Area. In the same letter he asked for a new cheque book and a replacement debit card, which were sent to 'Brian's new address', a mail drop in San Jose. In just a few weeks the criminal, who was never caught, had emptied Brian's account and run up a sizeable overdraft to boot.

The pros and cons of account takeover are straightforward. In its favour:

- 🔒 The account is already established, so there is no need to go through the bank's application process.
- 🔒 If the thief has picked an account with a reasonable credit rating it should be possible to realise a decent haul before the fraud is discovered. The US Federal Trade Commission reports an average take of $2,100 per victim for misuse of existing accounts, while in the UK the Association for Payment Clearing Services (APACS) reported the total losses from counterfeit or stolen cards, Card Not Present fraud and account takeover as £377.3 million in 2002.

🔓 Finally, with no real connection to the account the criminal can just walk away from it once the game is up.

The drawbacks of this technique are:

🔓 The thief doesn't really know how good the account will be until he starts using it – so his haul may be less than he hopes.

🔓 The fact that the legitimate owner of the account is using it at the same time makes early discovery more likely.

🔓 The short active life of each hijacked account means that the thief has to take over more of them more often. Many identity thieves practicing this version of the crime are caught because they source their information on each victim from the same place, creating a recognisable pattern that banks and law enforcement agencies know to look for.

Application fraud

The more sophisticated identity thief is not content to simply piggyback on one of your existing accounts. Instead he assembles a portfolio of the 'evidence of identity' detailed in the previous chapter and uses it to open a string of credit accounts in your name. When he defaults on the accounts he just walks away, leaving you with the bill.

♂ Victims left waiting for the other shoe to drop

In 1999 a retired US Air Force officer and his wife testified on identity theft before the Maryland State Legislature. Their story was one of multiple application fraud.

'This nightmare began in March 1997 when we received a phone call from Nations Bank in Norfolk, Virginia asking to speak to "John Doe". They wanted to know why I was delinquent in making payments on a 1996 Jeep Cherokee bought in Dallas, Texas. They were handling the account for a branch in Dallas, Texas that had been opened with them on October 16, 1996 to buy a Jeep Cherokee costing $27,424.'

Even though the couple had lived in Maryland for over 30 years, and never lived in Texas, the collection agency said they had their house under surveillance and had almost taken their car. Upon getting hold of a copy of the credit agreement the victims found that only the name and Social Security number were correct; the rest of the information – date of birth, address, etc – was not theirs.

The couple then requested copies of their credit reports from the three US credit reference agencies. They discovered that the criminals had taken out 33 fraudulent accounts in their names, for vehicles, credit cards, bank loans and more. The total came to a staggering $113,000.

The retired Air Force officer, who at the time was in his seventies, said: 'We have been affected both emotionally and physically by this fraud. This ordeal has taken three years out of our lives. It has cost us over $6,000 in attorney fees. It has delayed our move to South Carolina. There is always the feeling of waiting for another shoe to drop. We do not want the creditors for these fraud accounts to try to collect from our estate through a probate claim.'

So what are the pros and cons of application fraud? In its favour:

- As the story above shows, the total take from this type of crime can be significant.
- Because the accounts are run in parallel to the victims' own accounts, and from a different address, the fraud can run for much longer before the victim becomes aware of it.
- Finally, even when the victim does become aware, their details can still be recycled and used again, albeit at higher risk. There are cases of fraudsters opening accounts as fast as their victims can close them.

The drawbacks here are:

- The accounts are not readymade – the fraudsters must go through the whole application process.
- The financial magnitude of the crime can attract much more serious attention from law enforcement agencies. For example, in the US losses of the size described above could trigger a federal prosecution.
- The longer the scam runs, the higher the stakes get. And the fraudster never knows whether a fraud alert may have been placed on the victim's file.

As a part of the response to increased activity in the financial sector by both organised criminals and terrorists, opening accounts has become more difficult on both sides of the Atlantic. First the UK Money Laundering Regulations, intended to combat organised crime, became law in 1994. Then in the US the Patriot Act, aimed at fighting terrorism, was passed in 2001. Both of these laws require banks and other financial institutions to take steps to verify the identity of prospective customers who attempt to open accounts.

The US

Section 326 of the US Patriot Act (Uniting and Strengthening America by Providing Appropriate Tools Required to Intercept and Obstruct Terrorism Act of 2001) requires financial institutions to implement, and customers (after being given adequate notice) to comply with, reasonable procedures for:

- Verifying the identity of any person seeking to open an account to the extent reasonable and practicable;
- Maintaining records of the information used to verify a person's identity, including name, address and other identifying information; and
- Consulting lists of known or suspected terrorists or terrorist organisations provided to the financial institution by any government agency to determine whether a person seeking to open an account appears on any such list.

In practice this means that US financial institutions have had to implement Customer Identification Programs

(CIPs). Section 326 of the Act enumerates the types of identification required from customers to open an account:

- Name;
- Street address;
- Social Security number, tax identification number or other number from a government-issued identification document;
- Date of birth.

The types of documentary 'proof' of these identifiers include:

- Driver's licence;
- Passport;
- Other non-expired government-issued picture ID (if foreign, only documents recognised by US government).

However, acknowledging the fact that certain applicants may not have a passport or non-expired government-issued photo ID, some institutions will accept one of the following:

- Statement from a prior financial institution with current address and current utility bill with name and present address and a Social Security card;
- Non-expired government-issued photo ID card from a relative and proof of relationship (eg marriage certificate for husband/wife, birth certificate for parent/child, etc) and a Social Security card;

- Expired government-issued photo ID card and current utility bill with name and present address and a Social Security card;
- Textron ID with photo and number and current utility bill with name and present address;
- Other employer's ID with photo and number and current utility bill with name and present address and a Social Security card;
- Current school ID with photo and a Social Security card.

The two primary 'proofs' then are the driver's licence and the Social Security card.

The UK

Most banks, credit card issuers and other financial institutions require two forms of 'proof of identity'. These are required to be two separate documents, providing proof of identity and proof of address. The following lists are amalgamated from the requirements for three UK banks.

Proofs of name include:

- Current signed passport;
- *Current UK photocard driving licence (Provisional or Full);
- *Current full UK driving licence (old-style paper version);
- Current EU National Identity Card;
- Armed Forces Identity Card;
- Police Warrant Card;
- Photo student identification/matriculation card (from a recognised university or college);

- NHS medical card (customers 20 years old and under);
- Birth certificate (customers 20 years old and under);
- Firearms or shotgun certificate;
- Inland Revenue tax notification (not P45 or P60);
- Disabled driver's pass;
- OAP travel pass;
- National Insurance card supported by P60, P45 or payslip;
- Official Home Office status letter/IND registration card;
- *Bank/building society statement for an account showing your salary or pension credit;
- *Inland Revenue tax notifications (P60, P45, Notice of Coding);
- *Benefit agency letter;
- *Personal bank account cheque to open the account;
- Tax exemption certificate (C155, C156, SC60);
- Works identity card;
- Cheque guarantee/ATM/debit/credit card;
- *Pension book;
- *Child benefit book;
- *Disability benefit book.

Proofs of address include:

- Utility bill (within last six months);
- *Bank, credit union, building society, credit card statement or passbook (within last six months);
- Recent mortgage statement (within last 12 months);
- Current local council rent card or tenancy agreement (private tenancy agreements are not acceptable);

- *Benefit book (eg pension book) or benefits agency original notification letter;
- Vehicle licence renewal notification (V11);
- Vehicle registration document (V5);
- Home insurance certificate or policy;
- Motor insurance certificate or policy;
- TV licence renewal notification;
- University/college letter of acceptance/enrolment;
- Student Loan Company/LEA/SASS award letter;
- University/college letter of offer;
- Local Authority tax/rates bill;
- *Inland Revenue tax notification (P60, P45, notice of coding);
- Current mortgage statement or amendment notice;
- *Driving licence.

Items marked with an asterisk are present in both lists.

The apparent rigour suggested by these lists is misleading however. Because the government has made it clear to banks that no one in the UK should be denied access to a basic bank account, all UK banks are required to have an exception process, which can allow people to open basic bank accounts without providing the forms of ID usually required. Indeed journalists in the UK have reported being able to open a bank account using as little as a gas bill to 'prove' their identity.

Wholesale assumption of identity

This is the truly sinister end of the scale. Here the identity thief sets out to 'become you'. Starting with one or more breeder documents, usually a birth certificate and/or Social

Security number, he will apply for other official, often government-issued, forms of identification including a driver's licence and even a passport. These documents will be in your name, but feature his photograph and his version of your signature. The criminal will then go on to open accounts, apply for state benefits and so on. In the worst case he may commit serious crimes, leaving you to face the music.

🔓 The bargain basement ID store

In April 2003 a Special Weapons And Tactics (SWAT) team from the Reno, Nevada Police Department raided a house on the city's East side. Accompanying them were investigators from the Nevada Department of Motor Vehicles' Compliance Enforcement Division (CED). Prior to this CED investigators had arrested a man who was attempting to take out a $5000 loan, using a car as collateral. When questioned he identified the house where he had bought the fraudulent documents showing him as owner of the car. He claimed that a woman named Mel had sold him the complete package for $100.

Mel tuned out to be Melanie Marie Swearinger, who also went by the alias Jessica Megan Abend. The day-long search of her home turned up more than 100 fraudulent documents and an advanced computer system used to manufacture them. Using the birth certificate of a real person as her starting point, Swearinger manufactured and sold false drivers licenses, birth certificates, Social Security cards, automobile titles, registration slips and license plate numbers, CED investigators claimed. Investigators confiscated both fraudulent and authentic documents, the computer system and 45 compact discs containing images of documents from states across the country.

Swearinger, 24, was arrested on felony charges of forgery and possession and sale of false identification and on a misdemeanour charge of possession or use of another's birth certificate and two unrelated drug charges. She was booked into the Washoe County Jail.

🔓 The wanted criminal

In May 2004 detectives from the Vermont Department of Motor Vehicles Investigation Division arrested Robert Zmayefski on Cross Road in south Londonderry. Assisting DMV in making the arrest were representatives from the Vermont State Police, the Winhall Police Department and Special Agents from the Social Security Administration.

Zmayefski was arrested in connection with an identity theft. He was a fugitive from justice from Rhode Island and Massachusetts for various offences.

Charges were filed in Rutland County District Court for forgery, false impersonation, making material false statements on a license application and for being a fugitive from justice. Mr Zmayefski allegedly had obtained identity documents from Vermont DMV using an assumed identity in an effort to elude capture by law enforcement officials due to his fugitive status. A search warrant of Zmayefski's residence following his arrest aided in locating numerous items, including the birth certificate and Social Security number of the man he was impersonating. As a result of the search warrant, Zmayefski who was retuned to Rhode Island to finish his sentence there, may face federal charges for identity theft.

Identity thieves looking for quick financial gain will start with a living person. Those playing a longer-term game will, as we saw in the previous chapter, look for a dead victim:

♪ A classic case of ghosting

In July 2003 Special Agents from the US Department of State Diplomatic Security Service, together with several other federal agencies arrested Ronald D Moulton of Portsmouth, New Hampshire. Moulton was arraigned in US District Court in Concord, New Hampshire on a six-count indictment for identity theft.

Moulton allegedly used the birth certificate of a Maine boy who died two days after birth to obtain a New Hampshire driver's license, a US passport and to attempt to acquire a Social Security number by claiming the dead boy's birth certificate was his own.

DSS worked closely with the Social Security Administration Office of Inspector General, the Postal Inspection Service and the New Hampshire Department of Motor Vehicles to locate, identify and arrest the suspect.

Moulton faced a maximum prison term of ten years and possible fines of up to $250,000 for the passport fraud offence. Each of the other charges in the indictment carries up to a maximum five-year prison term and fines.

What are the pros and cons of wholesale ID theft? In its favour:

- 🔒 The fraudulent identity documents used by the criminal are above reproach as they are 'genuine' official government-issued documents.
- 🔒 If the victim is dead there is no need to share the identity and therefore less chance of discovery.
- 🔒 The scheme can be good for long-term impersonation.

The drawbacks are:

- 🔒 As with application fraud, new accounts need to be opened and security processes gone through.
- 🔒 Any negative factors (convictions, debts, etc) belonging to the victim follow the identity and can prove embarrassing to the thief.
- 🔒 If using a dead victim, the new identity appears from nowhere, with a corresponding need to establish history and biographical data, which can take time.

How identity thieves gather the information they need to commit their crimes

In chapter 1 I itemised the identifiers that criminals use to steal people's identities. So far in this chapter we've looked at some of the ways in which they use them. But how do they get their hands on these precious identifiers in the first place?

Identity thieves acquire the information they need through an incredibly wide range of techniques. But ultimately the sources of this information fall into two categories: the victims themselves and the people they trust.

No matter how closely we guard our personal identifiers we will always have to share them with others, from time to time, in order to function in society. Examples of the people we trust directly can include our employer, our bank or credit card company and our family and friends. In some cases trusted organisations such as banks will quite legitimately share this information with other organisations within the circle of trust, such as credit reference agencies. Many of these organisations will then outsource some of their data processing or other back-office functions to other companies who are also deemed to be trustworthy. By now the information that you may have provided to one trusted organisation has gone a long way, yet remained inside a secure, trusted environment. But, as the cliché goes, only the people you trust can betray you. Sometimes it's a straightforward betrayal, other times these firms have security that simply isn't up to the job of protecting our identities.

⚿ An inside job

In November 2002 the US Department of Justice announced what it believed to be the largest identity theft case in American history. Three men, Philip Cummings, Linus Baptiste and Hakeem Mohammed were arrested. Their massive identity theft scheme spanned nearly three years and involved more than 30,000 victims.

Cummings appeared in court facing a maximum term of 30 years imprisonment and a potential fine of $1 million or more for wire fraud and a maximum term of five years' imprisonment and a potential fine of $250,000 or more for conspiracy.

Cummings worked at Teledata Communications Inc (TCI), a company in Long Island that provided the computerised means for banks and other entities to obtain consumer credit information from the three commercial US credit history bureaus, Equifax, Experian and TransUnion. TCI provided software and other computerised devices to its client companies, which enabled them, through the use of confidential computer passwords and subscriber codes, to access and download credit reports of consumers for legitimate business purposes.

The prosecution alleged that, starting in early 2000, Cummings agreed to provide credit reports to a co-conspirator, 'CW' (who later became a cooperating witness in the investigation), in return for money. CW knew individuals who were willing to pay up to $60 per credit report, and it was charged that CW offered to split that money with Cummings. Thereafter, CW dealt with 20 or more individuals in the Bronx and Brooklyn who would bring lists of names and addresses and/or Social Security numbers and ask him to provide the relevant credit reports.

At some point in 2000 Cummings moved to Georgia, but he allegedly ensured that the scheme could continue first by travelling to New York to download the credit reports for CW and later by giving a pre-programmed laptop computer to CW on which he could download the reports himself. He also allegedly taught CW how to access the credit bureaus and download the reports.

According to the complaints, the individuals to whom CW sold the credit reports provided, in the aggregate, tens of thousands of names and hundreds of thousands of dollars to CW, which he split with Cummings. As a result of providing the credit reports, bank accounts holding tens of thousands of dollars in savings were depleted; credit cards were used without authorisation to the tune of thousands of dollars; address changes were made to accounts at various financial institutions; cheques, debit cards, ATM cards and credit cards were sent to unauthorised locations; and identities of victims were assumed by others.

James B Comey, US district attorney for the Southern District of New York, said 'With a few keystrokes, these men essentially picked the pockets of tens of thousands of Americans and, in the process, took their identities, stole their money and swiped their security. These charges and the potential penalties underscore the severity of the crimes. We will pursue and prosecute with equal vigor others who may be involved.'

Linus Baptiste was arrested on 29 October 2002 on a wire fraud charge related to the Cummings case. According to that complaint, phone numbers registered to Baptiste's residence were used to dial into Equifax's databases and download between 400 and 600 credit reports in August 2002. Credit reports, laptop computers and a document bearing Cummings' name were found in Baptiste's home.

In another related case involving fraud perpetrated on several of the victims, on 30 July 2002 a defendant using the name Hakeem Mohammed was charged with mail fraud in connection with an address change made to a line of credit opened by two of the fraud victims and the opening of accounts and lines of credit in the names of two other victims. Mohammed pleaded guilty to mail fraud and conspiracy charges on 2 October 2002.

Assistant Director in charge of the FBI's New York Field Office Kevin P Donovan stated: 'The defendants took advantage of an insider's access to sensitive information in much the same way that a gang of thieves might get the combination to the bank vault from an insider. But the potential windfall was probably far greater than the contents of a bank vault and, using 2lst-century technology, they didn't even need a getaway car. Using the same technology, we determined what was done and who did it, proving that technology is a double-edged sword.'

While consequences of identity theft can be devastating for the victim, there is rarely any personal malice on the part of the thief. But occasionally a betrayal closer to home can be very upsetting.

✆ Betrayed by his ex

John Stanley of Bidford-on-Avon, in Warwickshire was a victim of identity theft when his ex girlfriend decided to use his surname to gain credit.

Mr Stanley recalls: 'I have lived at my current address for over 20 years and worked really hard to ensure I have an excellent credit rating. But when I applied for a credit card from Goldfish to my amazement I was refused. This had never happened to me before so I didn't understand what the problem could be.

'I decided to apply for a copy of my credit file from credit reference agency Equifax, which revealed that my former girlfriend had applied for a £30,000 loan in my name. I was stunned because she'd left me seven years ago. As I understand, she had decided to start a new life abroad with her new partner and, because they were both already in debt, she used my name and address to obtain a loan for the deposit on their new house.'

Equifax advised Mr Stanley to apply for a Notice of Disassociation, which means lenders will see that he is no longer financially associated with his ex-girlfriend and any credit agreements she has. He also registered with CIFAS, the UK's fraud prevention service, which protects consumers from ID fraud.

Mr Stanley continues: 'It's terrifying to think that I would have been unaware of this debt until demands for money came through the door. I only found out because I was refused credit.'

Neil Munroe, external affairs director for Equifax said, 'When a relationship breaks down, it is always a stressful time and people don't want to worry about their financial situation as well. It is essential that individuals are aware of the financial risks a former partner poses, as Mr Stanley's story highlights.

'Although they had never shared a joint credit agreement, as they had been living together for a number of years they were automatically linked by same surname at the same address. Fortunately, Mr Stanley wasn't liable for the credit, but he was concerned that his former girlfriend could fraudulently use his address again in the future.'

Of course the vast majority of the people and organisations to whom we confide our personal data are decent, honest and wouldn't dream of betraying our trust. But they may not have any say in the matter when the identity thieves decide to go for outright theft, by means of a high-tech or brute-force attack on the computer system itself.

🔓 Computer criminal lived the high life thanks to his victims' tax returns

In June 2003 computer cracker Adil Yahya Zakaria Shakour, 19, of Los Angeles, California was sentenced by Chief Judge David F Levi to one year and one day in federal prison, a three-year term of supervised release and a $200 special assessment. Shakour was also ordered to pay $88,253.47 in restitution. In March of that year Hakour had pleaded guilty to committing fraud and related activity in connection with computers, and credit card fraud, in violation of 18 U.S.C. §§ 1030(a)(4), 1029(a)(2).

Court documents summarised that Shakour cracked into the following four computer systems during a thirteen-month period:

- On 26 and 27 April 2002, and 3 and 6 May 2002, a server at Eglin Air Force Base, a federal military base in Florida, during which he compromised the integrity of the system and defaced the website;
- On 5 May 2002, the computers of Accenture, a management consulting and technology services company, based in Chicago, Illinois;

- On 6 May 2002, an unclassified network computer at the Sandia National Laboratories in Livermore, California; and
- Between August 2001 and 10 May 2002, and also on 22 June 2002 and 10 September 2002, a computer of Cheaptaxforms.com, located in Mathews, North Carolina, which is a subsidiary of Pro Systems, Incorporated.

It is the fourth case that concerns us here. When entering his guilty plea, Shakour admitted gaining unauthorised access with the intent to obtain the credit card and personal information from the Cheaptaxforms.com website, which he then used to purchase items for his personal use. The credit card victims were located around the country, including Austin, Texas; Granada Hills, California; Colchester, Connecticut; Rockford, Illinois; Lenexa, Kansas; and Rockhill, South Carolina. Some of the items purchased included a ring valued at approximately $2,000; a bracelet worth about $1,500; and a necklace worth approximately $500; six two-way pagers; a Sony PlayStation 2; and miscellaneous computer parts (including ten network interface cards and two routers). Law enforcement officials contacted each victim who indicated the charges were not authorised.

The case was investigated by the Sacramento Valley Hi-Tech Crimes Task Force, and Federal Bureau of Investigation Sacramento Office with the assistance of the Los Angeles County District Attorney's Office and the US Attorney's Office for the Central District of California.

Cutting out the middle man

As the cases above show, centralised trusted repositories of personal information can be a valuable source of data for identity thieves. Once they gain access, they effectively have access to the identities of a vast number of people, which can mean massive rewards. But as with any investment, high returns don't come without high risks. All of the perpetrators discussed above were caught.

It's partly because of the high risk associated with these types of attack that many identity thieves prefer to go directly to the source. If setting out to steal someone's identity, where better to start than with the victim himself? The next few chapters examine in detail the common ways in which identity thieves get the information they need out of us, look at the ways in which they use it, and suggest simple tactics to foil their plans. But first we'll look what the law and businesses are doing to prevent identity theft.

The law and identity theft

Identity theft is one area where United States law is well in advance of the UK.

The 1998 Identity Theft and Assumption Deterrence Act made it a federal crime when anybody 'knowingly transfers or uses, without lawful authority, a means of identification of another person with the intent to commit, or to aid and abet, any unlawful activity that constitutes a violation of federal law, or that constitutes a felony under any applicable state or local law.'

The definition of 'means of identification' under the act is broad, and includes:

- Name;
- Social Security number;
- Credit card number;
- Cellular telephone electronic serial number;
- Any other piece of information that may be used alone or in conjunction with other information to identify a specific individual.

Offences under the Act are investigated by federal law enforcement agencies, including the US Secret Service, the FBI, the US Postal Inspection Service and SSA's Office of the Inspector General. Federal identity theft cases are prosecuted by the US Department of Justice. In most cases a conviction for identity theft carries a maximum penalty of 15 years imprisonment, a fine and forfeiture of personal property used in the crime.

Most importantly the Act recognises victims of identity theft as victims in the eyes of the law. Not only is it acknowledged that the criminal has committed an offence against the person whose identity is stolen, but also the victim is entitled to ask for compensation from the criminal for the harm done to them.

In July 2004, US President George W Bush signed the Identity Theft Penalty Enhancement Act (ITPEA), which provides for a mandatory two-year prison sentence for anyone caught in possession of another person's identity while committing a crime.

On top of this many states have identity theft laws, which provide additional protection and redress for victims.

In the UK however the law lags far behind. There have been numerous proposals to create an offence of identity theft. However, at the time of writing there is still no such crime. The most recent activity has been in the area of identity cards, based on biometric identifiers (which aren't foolproof, as discussed earlier), where draft government legislation addresses misuse of government-issued ID, and the Home Office proposals on Fraud Law Reform, which proposes a new offence of 'fraud by false representation'. These proposals do nothing to recognise the victim status of those whose identities are stolen. Furthermore, the Law Society has warned that any new offence, if drafted too broadly, runs the risk of criminalising ordinary privacy-enhancing behaviour currently taken for granted by many law-abiding citizens, such as checking into a hotel as 'Mr and Mrs Smith' or giving false details to avoid junk email.

Identity theft and business

In the US the Federal Trade Commission (FTC) has overall responsibility for combating identity theft. In addition many states have dedicated initiatives. The FTC has embarked upon a consumer awareness campaign and has also established several collaborative initiatives with law enforcement. Meanwhile many financial institutions have taken their own steps to address the problem. Most recently the three credit reporting companies (Equifax, Experian and TransUnion) launched an initiative to simplify the way victims notify them about the crime. Identity fraud victims can make one toll-free call to any of the nationwide credit reporting companies and the company contacted will share that information with the other two. Each company will follow a standardised three-step process to post a security alert on the credit file, opt the victim out of pre-approved offers of credit or insurance and mail the victim a copy of his or her credit file.

In the UK, despite there being no central law enforcement or government oversight of the problem, many financial institutions have taken steps to provide some assistance. APACS has attempted to educate consumers about identity theft. Furthermore the UK's consumer credit companies have established CIFAS to help identify and prevent fraudulent credit applications. CIFAS expanded its operations to provide a protective registration service that allows consumers who believe that personal identification documents may have been lost or stolen to preempt credit applications using their address by requiring lenders to seek further verification of the applicant's identity.

A CIFAS success story – David England

In 1998 David England was convicted of £1 million worth of fraud and sentenced to five years' imprisonment. England had spent several years travelling the country taking driving tests under assumed names. He used the driving licences obtained to open over 100 bank accounts, which he then nursed over a period of time, gradually building up the credit worthiness of each. To help with this England would register his assumed names on the electoral roll at rented drop addresses around the country.

Eventually one CIFAS member's suspicions were aroused when they noticed that all the credits to their account came from one bank and all the debits went to another bank.

The member issued a CIFAS Security Alert to ask other Members to check if they had any suspicious accounts at the addresses concerned. There were so many responses that the police were immediately asked to intervene. David England was arrested as he was about to leave the UK.

Chapter 3
Credit Card Cloning

Although this chapter talks about credit cards, much of the information also applies to debit cards. Indeed, many banking organisations don't even separate the two when compiling crime figures, simply referring to 'plastic card fraud' or just 'card fraud'. In this chapter I shall use the terms interchangeably.

🔓 The UK's biggest credit card fraud

In September 2003 three men were sentenced to a total of 17 years in prison for the UK's biggest ever credit card fraud. The gang, led by Sunil Mahtani, harvested credit card details from a financial services company, of which Mahtani's uncle was managing director, which processed payments for the airport rail service Heathrow Express. All together almost 9,000 identities were stolen and passed to forgers who created fake credit cards for use across Europe. By the time they were caught the three crooks and up to nine accomplices had used around 850 of the cards to steal over £2 million – much of it used to buy cigarettes in Belgium, which were then smuggled back into the UK to be sold on the streets. Had they been able to use all of the cards the figure could have been as much as £20 million. One of the gang told an undercover police officer that the credit card details came from collusive merchants who were 'prepared to go kamikaze'. Mahtani also admitted possession of child pornography with intent to distribute.

Statistically, credit card crime is the most common form of identity theft. A 2003 United States Federal Trade Commission survey of identity theft found that, in the preceding year, 67 per cent of identity theft victims, more than 6.5 million people, had suffered misuse of existing credit card accounts. In the UK, over £420 million was lost to plastic card fraud in 2002. Bankers group APACS estimates that one in three people has been a victim of card fraud.

In the majority of cases the victim's card is not stolen. The clever criminal knows better that to be caught with his hand physically in your pocket. Rather an identical copy, or clone, is manufactured, allowing the thieves to spend money from the victim's account while he or she is unaware that anything is wrong. Usually the theft is only discovered when the victim notices purchases they did not make on their statement. Increasingly however, banks' fraud detection units are developing more advanced methods of identifying the crime while it's in progress. They do this by looking for patterns of spending that match the common modus operandi of the criminals.

🔒 Richard's story

'I was on holiday in the US – Oregon to be precise. A day or so before I was due to return, I called into a local computer and electronics store to buy a couple of movies on DVD for the flight home. At the check-out the sales assistant said, "I'm sorry sir, your card has been rejected." Now I knew that I had plenty of room left on that card and asked him to run it again. Once again it was rejected. All of a sudden the penny dropped. I'd used the same card the previous day, in a local bookshop. That time the sales assistant said she had to call Visa. She then returned and asked me a lot of questions, like my date of birth and my postcode. I'd never been given the third degree while using a credit card before. After a trip back to the telephone she'd returned to the cash register saying, "That's fine sir, it's been authorised." At the time I thought it was some kind of random anti-fraud check. Now I know my card had been cloned.'

Richard's card had indeed been cloned. His bank had noticed a suspect pattern of spending and had put his card on a watch list while they tried to contact him. The purpose of the questioning was to confirm his identity.

'Back in the computer store I asked to speak to a supervisor. After some persuading he called Visa. The lady on the other end of the phone asked me more of the same kind of questions as the previous day and authorised the transaction. She also said, "I strongly advise you to contact your bank, they've been trying to get in touch with you," and gave me a telephone number in the UK.'

By now, as Richard's bank had been unable to get in touch with him, the status of his card had been escalated to the next level: declined but not cancelled. At a more serious level of escalation the sales assistant might have refused to return the card. At the most extreme level the police might have been called.

'I called the number the next day and was greeted with the words "Fraud department". After giving my card details and proving my identity for a third time I was asked, "Did you buy petrol in Watford on Tuesday?" Well I don't have a car and I'd been in the US for the past week. I explained this to the man, who said "Okay, we're going to have to cancel your card and issue another one, it'll be with you in five working days." He was very reluctant to give any details of what he thought had happened.'

One important thing to note here is the reference to buying petrol. Petrol is a favourite purchase for identity thieves with cloned cards, as we'll see later. But where did Richard stand now?

'Well, I didn't much like the idea of trying to get home without a credit card, in case of emergencies. After talking it through with the man from the bank he said that he'd set it up so that I could use the card if I had to, as long as I got the merchant to call Visa so that I could prove my identity, and that I should call the bank again when I got home. That was pretty much it really. I called the bank on my return and we went through the transactions on the card to work out which ones weren't mine. A few days later I got a new card and a few weeks after that a form to sign, listing the fraudulent transactions. The bank covered the cost of them so, touch wood, everything's okay.'

All in all, Richard was one of the luckiest victims of identity theft that I've encountered. Even though his bank had been unable to contact him, he did exactly the right thing when matters escalated. Jane's case was detected sooner, but the process wasn't as smooth.

Jane's story

'We received a letter from our credit card company asking us to contact them about some unusual spending activity. We gave them a call, but all the transactions they were concerned about seemed entirely normal, just our local food mart, drugstore and so on. The company did nothing further so we assumed that everything was fine.

'Two weeks later our statement arrived – things were far from fine. Our statement showed purchases apparently made with our card on the other side of the country. We called the company, who cancelled the card and refunded the money. But that wasn't the problem.

'We were due to go to Europe on holiday at the end of the week and needed the card, but the company said it would take ten days to get a new one to us. At one point we really thought we were going to have to cancel our trip. I was mad – why did they call me in the first place if they weren't going to do anything until it was nearly too late? In the end our local bank was able to arrange a card for us in three days. What a relief!'

Banks are understandably reluctant to discuss individual cases. In Jane's case the most likely explanation seems to be that the out-of-state transactions had triggered an alert on her account, but that human error led to the fraud investigator asking her about other, legitimate transactions. While this is unfortunate, the sheer number of card fraud cases happening today means that some mistakes are sadly inevitable.

Credit card cloning is not a simple matter. Unfortunately, the popularity of the crime means that a vast number of criminals know exactly how to go about it. There are three steps that the identity thieves must go through before living the high life on your line of credit:

1 Acquisition;
2 Manufacture;
3 Verification.

Acquisition

The first stage in the process is for the criminals to get hold of your credit card details. Sometimes these details are obtained from compromised customer databases (this is what had happened to Richard), or from collusive retailers. In most cases, however, they are obtained by a process known as 'skimming'.

Skimming

Take a look at your credit card. On the front you'll see a long 16-digit number, start and expiry dates and your name. On the back is your signature (I hope!) and a dark brown, black or sometimes gold or silver strip running the length of the card. This strip is made from much the same material as a cassette tape or floppy disc and contains all the information on the front of the card, recorded magnetically. When you use your card the sales assistant swipes it through a machine, which reads the information from the magnetic strip and uses it to process the transaction.

Skimming occurs when a sales assistant swipes your card through a second reader, known as a skimmer. These devices can hold the data from hundreds of different cards. Although once bulky devices, modern skimmers can be the size of a pager and attached inconspicuously to a belt. They are not hard to come by; a five-minute search on the internet will find vendors willing to sell them anonymously for as little as $350 and help and advice freely available on newsgroups. The more expensive models, such as the MP-CR from Magencoders (www.magencoders.com), come with an instant erase feature, which can destroy incriminating evidence.

Skimming can take place anywhere you part with your card. The most popular places are bars, restaurants and petrol stations – all places where your card is likely to be out of your sight while it is charged. Once the corrupt employee has swiped a sufficient number of cards he or she will sell them on up the chain. In the UK payment can be as little as £5 per card.

🔓 The Dutch connection

MasterCard received a complaint from a bank in the Netherlands. Several of the bank's customers had been victims of fraud after passing through City Airport in London, UK. It didn't take long for police to establish that every victim had visited the same restaurant within the airport terminal. Enquiries into the restaurant staff identified a suspect, Jay Heal, and after a short surveillance operation he was arrested. A card skimmer like the ones described above was found in his shirt pocket.

So far this appeared to be a standard case of skimming. The suspect worked in a restaurant, had access to customers' credit cards and had the necessary equipment. The choice of restaurant was interesting – by picking an airport Heal could be fairly certain that the customers would be paying by credit card and would most likely be foreign nationals. He may have felt that this offered him some additional measure of safety. He was wrong.

Following the arrest, police officers accompanied Heal to his flat, which they described as 'well appointed'. During the search Heal's flatmate James Dang walked in. Confronted with the police he spilled the beans, claiming that both men were Information Technology students at the University of East London, who were being paid £1,000 per month by a Chinese Triad gang to rent the flat and store items on their behalf.

A search of the premises revealed a further four skimming devices, several sheets bearing lists of credit card data, a quantity of skunk (a particularly potent form of cannabis), 1,000 ecstasy tablets, drug-dealing paraphernalia and 582 credit card numbers compromised at four different restaurants. It was also discovered that Dang had arrived in a stolen Porsche worth £35,000.

Here we see that the skimmers are on the bottom rung of a criminal ladder, this one allegedly controlled by the notorious Triads. Organised criminals rarely have only one iron in the fire, a fact confirmed by the drugs and the Porsche.

In July 2003 Heal and Dang were tried at Southwark Crown Court. Both pleaded guilty to conspiracy to defraud. Dang also pleaded guilty to possession of 1,000 ecstasy tablets with intent to supply and handling a stolen Porsche. On 29 July 2003, Jay Heal was sentenced to two years' imprisonment and James Dang to three years and nine months.

At the time of writing authorities have tracked the spending on 557 cards compromised by the two skimmers. For those 557 card numbers Heal and Dang would likely have received less than £3,000. Yet the total fraudulent spending identified so far on those same cards is over £400,000. Card cloning is clearly a very lucrative crime for some, if not for those at the bottom of the hierarchy.

Manufacture

Counterfeit cards fall into three categories. The most convincing ones are fully manufactured cards, printed in the bank's colours with the correct name and numbers embossed on the front and even a hologram. These cards will pass muster almost anywhere in the world. Again the equipment for this is readily available – prices start at $10,000, but the rewards can more than justify the costs. Industry sources talk of factories in East Asia producing 5,000 counterfeit credit cards in a single night and shipping them to Europe the next day in travellers' suitcases.

A less advanced method is to simply rewrite the information on the magnetic stripe of a stolen card that has been cancelled. Criminals using this method run the risk that a sales assistant may notice that the name and number on the printed voucher do not match those on the card. This appears to be a small risk, however, and one that many are willing to take. Some criminals have been known to partially 'remanufacture' these cards by using hot iron to smooth out the embossed card number and stamping tools to emboss the new number.

Criminals using the least sophisticated method do not attempt to counterfeit the appearance of a card at all. Instead the data is written to the magnetic stripe on a supermarket loyalty card or other freely and anonymously available card. Although these cards can only be used in machines and not with human beings the system has the advantage of very low entry costs. Writers such as the MAKstripe retail at around $750 at Escan (www.e-scan.com or www.escan-uk.com) and demonstration versions of computer programs to write or alter cards, such as RenCode2000, are freely available.

Verification

No matter how convincing the counterfeit card may look, the point of greatest risk for the criminal is when he attempts to use it. The information on the magnetic stripe may not have been recorded properly, preventing the card from working. Alternatively it may not match the name on the front of the card, due to a manufacturing error. Worst of all, the card may have been identified as having been cloned, or may even have been lost or stolen since it was skimmed. In this case, attempting to use the card could lead to arrest.

The prudent criminal therefore sets out to test the card in the safest way possible. Typically this will involve a machine-based transaction. Popular choices are buying a small amount of petrol from an automated pump or using a credit card-enabled payphone to make a short call. Once one or more such transactions are successfully completed the criminal will go on to milk the card for whatever he can, on average $3,000, testing it again periodically.

How to protect yourself

1   First and foremost: avoid letting your credit card out of your sight. Where possible stand in view of the credit card terminal the sales assistant will be using. Many restaurants now have central cash registers to which you can walk on your way out. Others have hand-held terminals, which your waiter can bring to your table.

2   If you use a restaurant where your card must be taken away, ask the manager to investigate putting a new system in place.

3   Make sure that your bank has your correct telephone number. If possible use a mobile/cell phone number and if not check messages left on your home phone. Richard's problems began because his bank was unable to contact him.

4   Finally check, re-check and check your statements again. Keep your receipts and compare them against your statement. It's far better to discover identity theft in your own home than to find yourself stranded without money in another country.

What banks and companies can do

As mentioned above, most banks now have fraud detection departments, which are developing increasingly accurate ways of identifying fraudulent card use. These computers, called intelligent fraud detection systems, constantly monitor spending on cards looking for unusual patterns.

Intelligent Fraud Detection Systems

Every time you make a credit card transaction the details are sent, via the credit card system operator, such as Visa or MasterCard, to the issuing bank. While authorising the transaction the bank runs it though a fraud detection system. These systems are based on a technology called 'neural networks', an advanced computer system that mimics a primitive brain. As you use your card this 'brain' builds a profile of your spending patterns. When your card is used to make a purchase this profile, together with a second profile based on known fraudulent card use, is used to determine whether the transaction is allowed or declined.

A typical known fraudulent pattern involves multiple purchases of easily resalable high-value items such as mobile telephones, consumer electronics items such as DVD players or stereos, and petrol. Sometimes the criminals will try to guess the floor limit of the store (the amount above which staff must seek authorisation before completing a transaction) and pitch the sale just under it. For higher value purchases, such as jewellery or computers, the criminals will work in partnership with a collusive retailer, who will turn a blind eye to a card that he knows to be fake. Other patterns that can trigger the system include excessive spending abroad and spending in multiple areas at the same time. Once an unusual pattern of spending is detected the bank can contact the cardholder to confirm that the transactions are genuine and put a block on the card if not. Of course this can be circumvented in cases of wholesale assumption of a victim's identity.

Of course no system is foolproof. One favourite tactic used by criminals is to wait for a holiday season. One manufacturer of intelligent fraud detection systems estimates that fraudulent spending can rise as much as 15 per cent over the holidays. During the holiday rush salespeople are often less vigilant. Together with the fact that our holiday spending is often very different from our day-to-day pattern, this can put a higher load on the banks' computerised cops, a load which they may find difficult to bear.

Working with retailers

Fraud-prone retailers and geographic areas are being identified and measures taken to help retail staff detect the use of counterfeit cards. This can include encouraging retailers to set a lower floor limit, offering rewards to staff who seize cards that are being used fraudulently and using ultraviolet lamps to identify counterfeit cards by checking for the presence of security information that is invisible under normal light.

Security codes

Many cards now carry a security code, known as a CSC or variously CVC, CVV2, CVC2 and CID. For Visa and MasterCard cards this number is three digits long, for American Express it is four digits long. The code is printed on the signature strip on the back of the card, but not encoded onto the magnetic strip and not embossed on the front. The skimmer could write it down but the problem is keeping his list in synch with all the cards he has skimmed, especially when the data is sold on up the chain. In theory this should stop skimming being effective. In practice, merchants are reluctant to use the code for fear of delaying or complicating transactions, thus running the risk of losing business to a competitor.

Chip and PIN/Smartcards

'Chip and PIN' is a new technology that banks hope will defeat most credit card fraud. The system is already in use in parts of Asia, Australia and South America and it is currently being rolled out in Europe. There is no date set for it entering the US, but debit cards in the US do use a PIN, rather than a signature, with just the magnetic stripe.

Each credit card that is a part of the 'Chip and PIN' scheme contains a tiny microchip connected to a grid made up of small metal pads. Instead of swiping the card through a magnetic stripe reader the sales assistant inserts the card into a device where metal pins make contact with the pads, allowing a computer inside the new reader to talk to the microchip. The microchip contains same information that is on the magnetic stripe.

Instead of signing a credit card slip, customers type a Personal Identification Number, or PIN, into the device, using a keypad similar to that on an ATM/cashpoint. The theory is that this makes it harder to clone credit cards as, while the fake card can have any signature the criminal wants, the PIN is known only to the legitimate card holder.

However Chip and PIN will not mean the end of credit card cloning for the following reasons.

Fraud abroad

A great deal of fraudulent card use takes place in other countries. Advances in technology and increasing access to international travel have made it easier than ever for organised criminals to move card information and even the cards themselves around the world. Recent figures show that around one third of fraud on UK cards takes place abroad, over half of that in France, Spain and the US. Most of the £130 million stolen abroad in 2002 was with card details obtained by skimming or other means. Given that Chip and PIN technology is used in only a few countries at present and that worldwide use of the technology is a long way off, there are still plenty of opportunities for fraudsters to clone cards in one country and use them in another.

The technological arms race

Although the banks claim that the technology is impossible to crack, history has shown that any new technological protection measure, no matter how well designed, is inevitably broken. Many of the vendors currently selling magnetic stripe equipment also offer products for working with smartcards (ie cards with chips). As Chip and PIN becomes more prevalent criminals will switch to using a combination of these new machines alongside techniques currently used for ATM crime, such as shoulder surfing (someone looking over your shoulder as you type your PIN). The TAMPER (Tamper And Monitoring Protection Engineering Research) Lab at the University of Cambridge Computer Laboratory has done theoretical research on ways of beating smart card security. For example, http://www.cl.cam.ac.uk/~mgk25/tamper2.pdf.

Card Not Present fraud

Chip and PIN does nothing to prevent Card Not Present fraud. When one crime becomes difficult criminals don't spontaneously reform. Instead they turn to a related, easier crime. As countries deploy Chip and PIN we can expect the criminals affected to switch to other methods, such as Card Not Present fraud.

PIN compromise

As we shall see in the next chapter, criminals have already developed a number of techniques for obtaining PINs for ATM cards. There is no reason to think that similar techniques will not be applied to Chip and PIN cards. In fact, banking security organisations have already anticipated an increase in attacks following the introduction of Chip and PIN and the 'subsequent rise in potential PIN compromise points from 40,000 (ATMs) to 850,000 (retail POS terminals)'.

Fallback

Whenever a new technology is deployed there is a transitional period when errors will occur. In order to avoid losing sales merchants must have the option of conducting a fall-back transaction. The UK's Chip and PIN programme defines a fallback transaction as 'one where the main or desired technology cannot be used, and a weaker technology has to be used to complete the transaction' and sets out what fallback transactions will be available, both during the roll out and once the technology is 'mature'. There are two types of fallback, 'technology fallback' and 'signature fallback':

🔒 Technology fallback – This occurs 'where the best card technology (chip or magnetic stripe supported by both card and terminal) cannot be used.' One example of an attack based on technology fallback is if clear nail varnish is used to cover the chip's metallic contacts – the reader would assume a chip failure and, if fallback is permitted, the merchant might then complete the transaction using the magnetic stripe and a signature.

🔒 Signature fallback – This occurs 'where the PIN cannot be used for what should be a PIN transaction.' This is also known as 'PIN Bypass'. The Chip and Pin literature talks of PIN Bypass in the context of a situation where the customer 'cannot remember their PIN or may temporarily be not able to enter their PIN'. In such cases the merchant may choose to offer PIN Bypass and allow the cardholder to sign the charge slip instead.

Although the Chip and PIN programme includes plans to phase out most types of fallback it is not clear when that will occur. Further, some types of fallback, such as 'Chip and Signature' cards for visually impaired people will remain. Even technology fallback merits the following statement acknowledging the possibility of its never being completely phased out: 'Once the mature situation is reached, technology fallback should not occur for domestic transactions. If it does, it is at merchant/acquirer risk (whereas for international transactions it will be at issuer risk subject to the usual conditions).'

Consumer and merchant resistance

A 2004 study of UK retailers found that only 53 per cent expect to be ready to use the new cards by January 2005, the deadline for implementation. Worse, migration to the new technology might not be complete until 2010. Twenty per cent of retailers cited lack of resources as a reason and many are putting off migration until their next regular hardware upgrade.

For consumers, resistance is more of a trust issue. Many people are concerned that the use of a PIN rather than a signature eliminates an essential audit trail, in that while a fraudulent signature may be demonstrated to be not that of the real account holder, a fraudulently entered PIN (obtained for example by shoulder surfing) is much more difficult to prove. Many UK activists are concerned that victims of fraud will be viewed as fraudsters themselves by banks anxious to maintain confidence in the security of their new system.

Chapter 4

Cashpoint/ATM Fraud

🔓 The policeman first robbed, then arrested

In late 1992 a policeman named John Munden returned home from a foreign holiday to find a substantial amount of money missing from his bank account. Some reports put the figure at £460, others say his bank account was empty. The money had been withdrawn from Automated Teller Machines (ATMs), also known as 'cashpoints' or 'cash machines'. Upon complaining to his bank, the Halifax Building Society (as it was then known), he was told that the bank had complete confidence in the security of its ATM network and he must therefore be mistaken. When he continued to complain his bank lodged a fraud complaint against him and, two years later in 1994, he was convicted of attempting to obtain money by deception. In fairness, it must be said that the Halifax insisted that the decision to prosecute was made by the Crown Prosecution Service, not itself. Eventually, after the intervention of expert witnesses and almost four years after the original complaint,

John Munden's conviction was overturned on appeal. The prosecution had been unable to prove that he was not a victim of ATM fraud. To this day, nobody has established how the money was stolen

The ATM or cashpoint has become a very popular target for criminals. Whenever we withdraw money from one of these machines we expose sensitive personal data, and criminals have developed a number of tricks to exploit this fact.

When we receive a new ATM card from our bank we go through a variant of the following security procedure.

1 The card and Personal Identification Number (PIN) are sent separately;

2 We are often required to acknowledge receipt of the card;

3 We are cautioned against ever carrying the card and a copy of the PIN together.

Notice the similarity between the first and third security measures. Their aim is to ensure that only the authorised user will ever have access to both the card and the PIN. This is because the card is a token and the PIN is an identifier. With possession of both of these the criminal can assume the account holder's identity, at least for the purpose of withdrawing money from any ATM.

🔓 Smalltown shenanigans

In May 2004 Roxanne and Michael Coffey visited an ATM in their hometown of Maryville, Tennessee to withdraw some cash on their way to dinner. Attached to the cash machine was a small device, along with a sign, which read: 'Due to recent fraud activity at this ATM you need to swipe your card below before getting cash.'

As they were in a hurry they followed the sign's instructions, but noticed that the reader wobbled as they used it. Their suspicions aroused, the Coffeys called the bank while still at the machine and were instructed to remove the device and the sign, which the bank, First Tennessee, later turned over to the FBI.

The Coffeys had just foiled an example of a crime that is growing ever more popular – the ATM attack.

In the same month, however, a victim on the other side of the Atlantic was not so lucky. Councillor Barry Dare, chairman of the North Cotswolds Police Authority, had £1,400 stolen from his account after using a cash machine that had been targeted by identity thieves. It was the second time that particular machine had been targeted, a previous victim having had £7,500 stolen.

Both Cllr Dare and the Coffeys said that while they expected this type of crime to happen in big cities they were shocked to encounter it in a small town.

ATMs have been around for a long time. Most of us use them every week. Indeed many of us even use ATMs in other countries without a second thought. At the end of

September 2003, APACS reported there were over 45,000 ATMs in Britain and the number continues to rise. ATMs in the UK dispensed £136.4 billion in 2002 in 2.5 billion transactions, with an average cash withdrawal of £60. The ATM Industry Association estimates that there are over 1.2 million ATMs in use worldwide. The figure for the US alone is put at 371,000. Our familiarity with ATM networks has arisen in part because they are so convenient, allowing us access to cash at any time, regardless of bank opening hours or distance from our branch. However that very familiarity often breeds a contempt for basic security precautions, which criminals exploit to relieve us of our identities.

There are two parts to a successful assault on our ATM privileges by the criminal: obtaining the account information on the ATM card and obtaining the PIN. The criminal may use a combination of the tactics listed below, or a combined method.

Obtaining the account information
- Physical theft of the card;
- Theft of the card by machine tampering;
- Theft of account information by machine tampering;
- The 'card cleaner'.

Obtaining the PIN
- Theft of written record;
- Shoulder surfing;
- The 'helpful stranger';
- Remote camera;
- Local camera;
- Keypad overlay.

Combined methods
- 🔒 Machine takeover;
- 🔒 Inside job.

Obtaining the account information
Physical theft of the card

A criminal can steal your ATM card by any number of means, many of them familiar to us: picking pockets, mugging, snatching a handbag, burglary, theft from a motor vehicle, and so forth. In the past decade, however, victims have been reporting a new technique, the so-called 'dropped money' scam.

🔓 Michael's story

I was using a cashpoint near my office. It was the type where you insert your card and the machine gives it back at the end of the transaction. Just after I'd pushed the buttons to make a withdrawal the man behind me in the queue pointed to the ground at my feet and asked whether I'd dropped some money from my wallet. I looked down and sure enough there was £10 lying at my feet. I picked it up, uncertain as to whether or not it was mine and intending to check, and returned my attention to the machine. My money was there, but there was no sign of the card. Nor of the fellow behind me.

This is a low-tech crime that has been happening for some years. In this case, the man behind Michael in the queue was a criminal. He dropped the £10 himself and used the moment of distraction while Michael bent down to pick it up to snatch his victim's ATM card as soon as it was ejected.

Theft of the card by machine tampering

Known in Europe as the 'Lebanese loop', card trapping devices are usually thin pieces of plastic, often with a loop of thin film, that are inserted into the card slot of the ATM. When a customer inserts their bankcard, this device causes two things to happen. First it prevents the ATM from properly reading the card, causing a PIN verification failure. Second, it prevents the machine from either ejecting or retaining the card. Sometimes the Lebanese loop may take the form of a narrow plastic strip with a false ATM card slot attached. There have even been reports of criminals using a length of magnetic tape, such as that found in a videocassette.

Having inserted the device into the ATM, the criminal will loiter near it. Upon seeing a customer approach the machine, he or she may line up behind their victim, as if intending to be next to use the machine. Because the plastic slip blocks the machine from reading the card the victim will get no response, no matter what keys they strike. Eventually the customer gives up and either leaves the area or enters the establishment operating the machine to complain. At this point the criminal removes the device from the ATM, along with the card.

Skimming – theft of account information by machine tampering

While the method above will only work with the type of ATM that 'swallows' the card, skimming can be used with many other ATMs too. The criminal affixes an electronic card reader to the machine, in such a way that the ATM card must pass through the criminal's reader as well as the machine's. This may take a number of forms, ranging from a small, stand-alone device affixed to the card slot to a complete new fascia. The device reads and records the data on the magnetic stripe of the bankcard. The criminal either returns to retrieve the device or downloads the data by radio from a nearby car. A new card is then manufactured using the information recorded from the magnetic stripe. Again this happens in much the same way as for credit and debit cards in shops, etc. It should be pointed out, however, that for ATM cards that will only ever be presented to a machine, the manufacturing cost per card can be significantly lower than for cards that may have to pass human scrutiny.

The 'card cleaner'

This method of stealing your account information works with all ATMs, even those designed to be tamper resistant. This is because it relies upon the gullibility of the victim for its success. The criminal simply affixes a small device to the machine or to an adjacent wall, and puts up a sign requesting customers to use the 'card cleaner' before presenting their card to the ATM. Of course the card cleaner is nothing of the sort – it is in fact just another magnetic stripe reader, harvesting the account details of customers gullible enough to fall for the scam.

The Coffey's story earlier was a variation on this scam. Another is attaching the skimming device to the card reader used for unlocking the lobby door, in cases where banks have placed their ATMs in a lobby for greater security.

Obtaining the PIN

The techniques listed above only give the criminal half of the puzzle. Without the Personal Identification Number the card, or the information harvested from the magnetic stripe, is to all intents and purposes useless. Criminals have therefore developed a number of ways of obtaining your PIN.

Theft of written record

While this is the most obvious method, it is usually only used when the criminal physically steals the card too. This is why banks advise against writing down your PIN and in particular against keeping it with the card.

Shoulder surfing

Here the criminal pretends to be another customer at the ATM, queuing up behind the victim. While the victim enters his or her PIN number the criminal will look over their shoulder, memorising the PIN. This technique is used most often with the 'dropped money' technique. With the machine tampering attacks such as the Lebanese loop, often the thieves will place a sign on the ATM instructing customers to re-enter their PIN a number of times should the machine 'malfunction', which is actually to ensure they can memorise it. In a new variation on this old method, criminals are now using cell phone cameras to capture the PIN.

The helpful stranger

A variation on shoulder surfing, this approach is used with the Lebanese loop. Again the criminal pretends to be another customer. In this case he waits until the victim encounters an irregularity, namely the machine's failure to process the card. At this point the criminal steps forward, offering helpful advice along the lines of 'Oh, this happened to me a couple of days ago. I got my card back by typing in my PIN again and hitting "clear" twice. I think there's something wrong with the machine.' The victim, now taking advice from the helpful stranger, is off his guard and it is even easier for the criminal to observe his PIN.

♂ His victims thought he was trying to help

In June 2003 Roberto Inzitari, a 36-year-old landscape gardener from Daytona Beach, Florida pleaded guilty to stealing more than $97,000 at ATMs in Maryland, North Carolina, South Carolina, Florida and Washington DC over a period of eight to nine years.

The court, in Fairfax, Virginia heard that Inzitari would target an ATM by inserting a Lebanese loop into the card slot and then loitering in the area. When a victim's card became trapped, Inzitari would approach and claim that the same machine had jammed up with his card the previous day and that the victim might be able to get their card back by reentering their PIN. Of course, Inzitari would watch and memorise the PIN, then, once the victim had left, remove the card and use it, together with their PIN, to raid their account.

Remote camera

The problem for the criminal with the above two techniques is that he might arouse suspicion by repeatedly queuing at the same ATM. With the remote camera trick, the thief loiters nearby but out of sight, perhaps in a vehicle or building across the road. He trains a video camera on the ATM and films the victim or victims entering their PIN. This approach is used with machine tampering attacks, and can also be used with the Lebanese loop and 'dropped money' scams as part of a two- or three-criminal operation.

Local camera

Here we have the most high-tech technique for obtaining victims' PINs. One or more tiny pinhole cameras are attached to the ATM, either unobtrusively in a corner of the machine or concealed inside a fake leaflet holder. These days the cameras are most often modern wireless models, transmitting the video by radio to the criminal or an accomplice in a nearby building or car.

Keypad overlay

Sometimes called a 'ghost' overlay, these are fake numeric pads that are placed over the genuine keypad on the ATM. When the victim keys in their PIN it is recorded by the device. The most advanced version is made of thin transparent material, which actually allows the machine to function normally and is far more difficult to detect. These devices are usually used in conjunction with skimmers.

🔓 An Australian case

In August 2003, Kok Meng Ng, 29, pleaded guilty to defrauding more than AUS$623,000 from bank customers by planting electronic skimmers and wireless cameras on 36 ATMs in Sydney, Australia. Sunil de Silva, prosecuting, said Ng was part of a gang that attacked the bank accounts of 315 victims, generally withdrawing less than AUS$1000 at a time. In all, Ng pleaded guilty to federal charges carrying a maximum five-year jail sentence, and computer crime charges carrying up to a three-year sentence.

With the ATM card or magnetic stripe data gained from one of the first set of techniques and the PIN obtained through a technique from the second set, the criminal now has everything required to make the maximum possible withdrawal from the victim's account. ATM card skimming is perhaps the worst type of attack because the victim has no idea that anything has happened. In a relatively short space of time clones of the victim's ATM card can be sent anywhere in the world, maximising the potential loss. However there are a number of relatively simple steps that can be taken to guard against becoming a victim of one of these approaches, as we shall see later in this chapter.

The combined methods

The combined methods are much more difficult, and perhaps even impossible, for consumers to guard against, although there are steps that can be taken by financial institutions to limit the damage.

Machine takeover

In December 2003 US Secret Service Agents posing as maintenance men arrested a man at a motel in Michigan.

According to an indictment filed in May 2003 the man, with accomplices, bought and installed a network of up to 55 ATMs in New York, California and Florida. The man, who is alleged to have links to Albanian-Yugoslav organised crime, installed skimming devices in his ATMs, harvesting card details and PINs from over 21,000 people and stealing over $3.5 million in a two-year period.

The gang placed their ATMs in convenience stores, enticing the owners of the stores to switch to using their machines by offering them higher fees. One merchant reported being offered $1.75 per withdrawal as opposed to the $1 he was receiving from his current machine. While suppliers claim to have tightened up their controls on who can buy an ATM, it is notoriously difficult to achieve a 100 per cent success rate in any security initiative.

Inside job

Although I know of no recorded convictions where a member of staff at a bank was found to have used their position to match a PIN to an account, researchers at Cambridge University have demonstrated methods that would allow a corrupt insider to gain access to PINs.

How much cash can they take?

Most ATM cards have a daily withdrawal limit. You could therefore be forgiven for assuming that the criminals could only get that amount per day. In fact you'd be wrong. Criminals have come up with a couple of schemes to maximise their take from ATMs.

Timing

Although most cards have a daily limit, the withdrawal allowance is often reset at midnight each day. Ken Cooper, a product marketing manager for Gasper Corporation, a provider of ATM management software, notes that thieves targeting ATMs frequently work around midnight, so that they can withdraw the maximum amount of cash allowed for two days rather than just one.

Reversal fraud

Transaction reversal fraud is a very sneaky trick that can allow a criminal to withdraw massive amounts of money from a single account in a single day. The technique itself is simple. Having obtained a card and PIN the thief makes a withdrawal from an ATM, asking for the maximum amount. When the money is ejected, however, instead of taking the lot the criminal holds a note or two in place and removes the rest, usually from the middle of the pile of notes. This leaves some money still in the slot. Now the criminal waits. After a short time the ATM will draw the remaining money back into the slot, sending a 'time out' error message to the financial institution. Because the ATM cannot usually count the number of notes drawn back in it thinks that the whole amount of the withdrawal has been recovered. This often causes the transaction to be reversed on the cardholder's account, meaning that the same card can be used again and again to withdraw more money. CUNA Mutual group reports losses of up to $26,000 through this technique.

How to protect yourself

There are a number of steps you can take to safeguard against cashpoint/ATM crimes.

Your PIN

Never carry your PIN with your ATM card. Some people who feel that they must make a note of their PIN disguise it by hiding it in the middle of a telephone number, a date or some other string of numbers. But even then they should never carry it with their card. This strategy is risky at best, as the following story from the Financial Ombudsman Service shows:

♪ Customer kept note of PIN

When Mr S's wallet was stolen, he reported the loss of his American Express and Visa cards, but forgot about his cash card. By the time he remembered and reported it to the firm – the following day – four withdrawals, each for £250, had been made. These withdrawals were made very close together – just before, and just after, midnight.

The transaction listing showed that, before the first withdrawal was made, there had been an unsuccessful attempt when the wrong PIN was entered. And there was another unsuccessful attempt after the second withdrawal, because the daily withdrawal limit of £500 had, by then, been reached.

Mr S accepted that he had kept a written note of his PIN in his wallet, but said that it had been 'disguised'. No one doubted that he was the victim of fraud. But who was liable for the withdrawals? The Banking Code limits customers' liability to £50 for withdrawals made before a lost or stolen card has been reported missing provided (amongst other things) that a note of the PIN was not made on the card, or kept near it.

Because Mr S rarely used the card, and because the thief was able to make the withdrawals after only one failed attempt, we decided Mr S had kept a note of the PIN near to the card in an undisguised or poorly disguised form. The firm was therefore entitled to debit his account with the four withdrawals.

Choosing your ATM

1   Pick your ATM carefully. Always remember your personal safety is the most important thing.

2   Where possible, use ATMs you're familiar with. This will make it more likely that you'll notice anything different about the machine, such as the addition of a skimming device or a camera. If you notice anything unusual, do not use the machine and report it to the bank as soon as possible.

3   ATMs located inside businesses and in business-hours branches, and machines with security cameras are less likely to attract criminals.

Using the ATM

4   Be alert to the people near you. Watch out for shoulder surfers or anybody you feel is standing too close to you.

5   Before inserting your ATM card, run your thumb along the length of the card slot. The Lebanese loop has a couple of small protrusions, used by the criminal to gain purchase when removing it. If you feel these protrusions then it is likely that the ATM has been tampered with and you should not insert your card.

6 Don't use the card cleaner! ATMs don't have these, ever, so it can only be a skimming device.

7 If you feel uncomfortable at any point, cancel your transaction and walk away.

8 Stand close to the machine and always obscure the keypad with your body or your other hand when entering a PIN.

9 Never allow yourself to be distracted. The dropped-money scammers rely on this moment of distraction.

10 Do not accept help from 'well-meaning' strangers, especially if you experience difficulties with your transaction (such as your card being 'eaten' by the machine) and they advise you to enter your PIN again.

Leaving the ATM

1 Once you have completed your transaction, discreetly put away your money and card before leaving the ATM.

2 If the ATM does not return your card, report its loss immediately to your bank.

3 Dispose of any ATM receipt, mini-statement or balance enquiry with care. Take them home to do it, and treat them like any other sensitive document.

4 Keep a close eye on your monthly statement, as well as your balance, and report any surprises to your bank.

A note on liability

While legislation does limit the liability of customers for fraudulent ATM withdrawals, that limitation is not absolute.

In the UK the Banking Code places the following responsibilities on the customer, in Section 12.4:

- 🔒 Do not allow anyone else to use your card, PIN, password or other security information.
- 🔒 If you change your PIN you should choose your new PIN carefully.
- 🔒 Always learn your PIN, password and other security information, and destroy the notice as soon as you receive it.
- 🔒 Never write down or record your PIN, password or other security information.
- 🔒 Always take reasonable steps to keep your card safe and your PIN, password and other security information secret at all times.
- 🔒 Keep your card receipts safe and dispose of them carefully.
- 🔒 Never give your account details or security information to anyone unless you know who they are and why they need them.

Subject to those conditions, customer liability for losses is then set out as follows:

12.9 If you act fraudulently, you will be responsible for all losses on your account. If you act without reasonable care, and this causes losses, you may be responsible for them. (This may apply if you do not follow section 12.4.)

12.10 Unless we can show that you have acted fraudulently or without reasonable care, your liability for the misuse of your card will be limited as follows:

- If someone else uses your card before you tell us it has been lost or stolen or that someone else knows your PIN, the most you will have to pay is £50.
- Someone else uses your card details without your permission for a transaction where the cardholder does not need to be present, you will not have to pay anything.
- If your card is used before you have received it, you will not have to pay anything.

In other words, writing down your PIN or being careless with it could leave you liable for the whole amount stolen from your card.

In the US the question of how quickly you make your report is also a factor. The Electronic Fund Transfer Act, which provides consumer protection for ATM withdrawals, lists the following three liability bands:

- If you report your ATM card lost or stolen within two business days of discovering the loss or theft, your losses are limited to $50.
- If you report your ATM card lost or stolen after the two business days, but within 60 days after a statement showing an unauthorised electronic fund transfer, you can be liable for up to $500 of what a thief withdraws.
- If you wait more than 60 days, you could lose all the money that was taken from your account from the end of the 60 days to the time you reported your card missing.

What banks and companies can do

Banks and ATM manufacturers are already working to enhance the security features of ATMs. However the massive number of ATMs in use (over 45,000 in Britain by 2003 and over 550,000 worldwide in the Visa Global ATM Network alone) means that, no matter how secure the new machines are, criminals will still have access to plenty of the old-style machines, with all their vulnerabilities.

Furthermore, in the UK APACS has warned ATM operators to expect an increase in attacks against the ATM network following the roll out of 'Chip and PIN', which will increase the number of 'potential PIN compromise points from 40,000 (ATMs) to 850,000 (retail POS terminals).'

With that said, some of the new security features can be fitted retroactively to older machines. For example, ATM manufacturer Wincor Nixdorf has developed a special module for its ProCash ATM. This device has sensors that permanently monitor the ATM's card slot. If a foreign device is detected the machine can be taken out of service. Other manufacturers have developed similar devices.

Closed Circuit Television (CCTV) monitoring of ATMs can deter criminals and increase arrest rates. Indeed one of the first breaks in the case of the gang who bought their own ATMs, mentioned earlier in this chapter, came when one of the gang was caught by surveillance camera at a legitimate ATM making one transaction after another.

Intelligent Fraud Detection systems or other analysis, similar to that used for credit card transactions, could alert customers to unusual patterns of withdrawals. Also many forms of ATM tampering leave a noticeable electronic trail, according to Gasper Corporation, a manufacturer of ATM management software. For example, a high number of repeated card reader errors at a single ATM can indicate a Lebanese loop-style card trap, Gasper claims. These techniques can also be used to combat reversal fraud.

There is a need to maintain more stringent security criteria over who can own or operate an ATM. It's true that many of the companies that supply ATMs have tightened their customer vetting procedures, but when you remember that we're talking about identity theft it should come as no surprise if criminals turn up with sophisticated bogus identities in an attempt to evade the checks.

Banks and police have found that by simply marking a 'privacy zone' or 'defensive space' around an ATM, customers become more aware of their surroundings and the likelihood of shoulder surfing or distraction attacks is reduced.

Finally, if ATMs were to record some kind of unique 'flag' on the magnetic stripe of the card that changes every time the card is used, it would only be a matter of time before the real card and the counterfeit one are out of synch. After the original card is skimmed, whichever card is used first would be able to function normally until the other card is used. The machine would detect the incorrect flag and both cards could be blocked. One simple way of doing this would be to record the location and date of the transaction. The drawbacks to this scheme are the need to upgrade the installed base of existing equipment and the increased transaction time and data transfer requirements of such multiple checks.

Chapter 5

Card Not Present Fraud

Also known as 'fraudulent possession of card details', Card Not Present fraud occurs when criminals use your credit card details to make fraudulent Card Not Present transactions. Card Not Present transactions can, in themselves, be perfectly legitimate. Whenever we pay a bill or buy goods or services over the telephone, by fax, mail order or on the internet we are engaging in a Card Not Present transaction. Within the payment cards industry this is often referred to as the mail order/telephone order (MOTO) arena. However, the lack of face-to-face contact and the fact that there is no need to manufacture a card makes Card Not Present fraud very attractive to criminals. APACS puts the UK cost of Card Not Present fraud at £110.1 million in 2002, up 15 per cent from the 2001 figure of £95.7 million and a massive increase over the cost in 1998 of £13.6 million. Peter Dorrington, head of fraud solutions at software company SAS UK, predicts a further increase as Chip and PIN technology is rolled out to the high street.

🔓 Emma's story

Emma, a 26-year-old public relations account manager from London, had held her debit card for seven years without any problems. That is, until the day she tried to book some aeroplane tickets for a holiday and found that there were insufficient funds in her account. When she checked with her bank she found that £399 had been charged to her account for an online electrical equipment purchase – a purchase she had not made. The bank cancelled her card and sent her the usual fraud declaration forms, and eventually the money was refunded. While she still doesn't know for certain how the fraudster got her account details, Emma does admit that throwing out receipts in her rubbish may be the source. 'I'm now much more alert to how this type of fraud can happen,' says Emma. 'I examine my statements very carefully and I also now thoroughly destroy statements and receipts when I've finished with them. I'm also in the habit of getting in touch with my bank once a week for a description of recent transactions going through my account.'

While Emma's card had not been cloned, a criminal or criminals had still used it to buy goods. Somehow, they had obtained the information on the card and used it over the internet for a Card Not Present transaction.

At the most basic level, all the criminal needs is your name, credit card number and expiry date. This information can be obtained from a number of sources:

Skimmed cards

All the information collected for credit card cloning can be used to commit Card Not Present fraud – it saves the money, time and effort involved in manufacturing the counterfeit card.

Discarded receipts

Many credit card or store receipts carry the full card number, along with all the other details – name, expiry date, etc – that the criminal needs to make a Card Not Present transaction. This can be useful – I myself have bought an item over the telephone, despite having left my wallet at home, simply by reading back the information printed on one of my own card receipts, which happened to be in my pocket. Despite the risks, however, many of us still throw these receipts away with no thought as to the potential risk.

Carbons

Less common in these days of electronic transactions but still viable, the old manual card swipe machines use slips of carbon paper to transfer the imprint to all pages of the credit card slip. Identity thieves sort through the business's rubbish (a practice called 'bin raiding' or 'dumpster diving') to find these carbon paper slips and copy down the details.

Card number generation

Computer programmes that generate sequences of credit card numbers from valid Bank Identification Numbers (BINs) – the first few digits of your credit card number that identify which bank issued it – are widely available over the internet. Of course while these numbers may be valid they will not necessarily have been issued yet. And then the criminal still has to deal with guessing the expiration date. There are, however, cases of people finding that their card has been compromised by just such means.

Traditionally, Card Not Present fraud happened by telephone or mail order. Today, criminals are increasingly moving to the internet. Certain newsgroups and internet relay chat (irc) channels feature discussions of card number generators and the specifics of the vulnerabilities of many e-commerce engines used by websites to process transactions. Typically the fraudsters will buy laptop computers or similar products with a high resale value. Mobile phones are another of the fraudsters' favourite purchases.

Sue's story

Sue had been thinking of getting a cellular phone – until an identity thief got there first. The man set up a cell phone account in his name and paid two bills using Sue's debit card number and the phone company didn't bat an eyelid.

This was a classic case of Card Not Present fraud. The thief had somehow obtained Sue's debit card number, possibly from a discarded receipt or statement, and used it to set up a new account over the phone. First Sue called her bank and made a fraud report. Then, she says: 'I called the phone company and had them trace the phone account using my Visa/debit number. A telephone operator told me the account's owner was a man, and said he set up the account more than two months ago. I asked his name and was told the information was private.'

Sue made a police report. When her bank opened, she called them again, and was told that the fraud report wouldn't come across anyone's desk for a few days.

Eventually Sue closed her account and opened a new one. She called her credit card issuers and asked that ID be required for every purchase. That evening she used a card and was not asked for ID. It's easy to understand why she wearily says, 'From this experience, I've learned that information is only private when you're a-law abiding citizen; everyone else has free reign.'

How to protect yourself

Beyond the steps outlined in previous chapters, there is very little you can do to protect yourself. But there is one important measure you can take.

Guard your receipts

Check your receipts carefully and destroy rather than discard them. Even if the merchant has truncated your credit card number to only four digits, you may still be vulnerable. This is because in many places there is no clear standard among merchants specifying which four digits should be printed. So, while one may only print the last four digits another may print one of the middle two blocks of numbers. The numbers on one receipt fill in the blanks on another. Thus an identity thief with several receipts or credit card slips to work from could reconstruct your credit card details from the partial information on each slip.

A report, released in 2003 by the APACS Card Watch initiative, found that many cardholders in the UK still ignore the most basic security precautions when using their cards:

- 🔒 More than one in three never shreds or burns their bank or credit card statements (37 per cent) or receipts (35 per cent) when they are finished with them;
- 🔒 One in five (19 per cent) has let others use their card to make purchases over the internet, by mail order, by phone or by fax;
- 🔒 One in five (19 per cent) checks their bank and credit card statements only sometimes, rarely or never; and
- 🔒 One in six (17 per cent) is unconcerned at letting their card out of their sight when shopping.

What banks and companies can do

They can do a great deal more than at present! Card Not Present merchants are liable for chargebacks. This means that if a Card Not Present transaction is found to be fraudulent the person who sold the product must carry the cost. This gives them a strong financial incentive to take precautions although, sadly, many reports claim that take up of security measures among Card Not Present merchants is lower than might be hoped.

Banks and card issuers have created a number of verification tools to assist merchants when processing Card Not Present transactions. These include:

Address Verification Service (AVS)

If the criminal has obtained your card details from a receipt, or indeed from most sources other than your statement, then it is unlikely that he will know your real address. Therefore, when asked to provide the billing address for the card he is most likely to provide a false or fictitious address. AVS compares the numbers in the billing address entered with those in the address on file with the card issuer. This takes place as part of the authorisation process, giving the merchant an opportunity to weed out fraudulent transactions. AVS is not foolproof, however. If the criminal knows the victim's address then AVS will not provide any impediment to the crime. Even in cases where the criminal does not know the address, inconsistencies in implementation and incompatibilities between the AVS systems used by different banks and in different countries, together with lack of take up by Card Not Present merchants, mean that AVS is far from 100 per cent reliable.

Card Security Code (CSC)

Also known by, for example, Visa as the Card Verification Value 2 (CVV2), this is a three or four-digit number printed on the signature panel on the reverse of the card. Because this is not stored on the magnetic stripe or printed on receipts or statements it is far more difficult for a criminal to gain access to this number without having the card.

Other schemes

Some card issuers operate additional security schemes targeted at internet-based Card Not Present transactions. For example Verified by Visa and MasterCard SecureCode ask the customer to enter a password to confirm their identity before authorising the transaction. A number of third-party solutions are also on the market.

Be alert for obvious signs of Card Not Present fraud

There are also a number of indicators that, while not being proof of fraud, should ring alarm bells if they appear together. The following list is provided by Visa:

🔒 First-time shopper – Criminals are always looking for new victims.

🔒 Larger-than-normal orders – This requires knowledge of what a 'normal-sized' order is. Because stolen cards or account numbers have a limited life span, crooks need to maximise the size of their purchase.

🔒 Orders consisting of several of the same item – Having multiples of the same item increases the criminal's profits.

🔒 Orders made up of 'big-ticket' items – These items have maximum resale value and therefore maximum profit potential.

🔒 Orders shipped 'rush' or 'overnight' – Crooks want these fraudulently obtained items as soon as possible for the quickest possible resale, and aren't concerned about extra delivery charges.

🔒 Orders shipped to an international address – A significant number of fraudulent transactions are shipped to fraudulent cardholders outside the merchant's country.

🔒 Transactions on similar account number – This is particularly useful if the account numbers being used have been generated using software available on the internet (eg CreditMaster).

🔒 Orders shipped to a single address but made on multiple cards – These could also be characteristic of an account number generated using special software available on the internet, or a batch of stolen cards.

🔒 Multiple transactions on one card over a very short period of time – This could be an attempt to 'run a card' until the account is closed.

🔒 Multiple transactions on one card or a similar card with a single billing address, but multiple shipping addresses – This could represent organised activity, rather than one individual at work.

🔒 For e-merchants, multiple cards used from a single Internet Protocol address – More than one or two cards would well indicate a fraud scheme.

🔒 Orders from internet addresses making use of free e-mail services – For these services, there are no billing relationships and often no audit trail or verification that a legitimate cardholder has opened the account.

APACS make a similar list available, along with guidance for merchants at http://www.cardwatch.org.uk/pdf_files/cnp_pack.pdf.

🔒 Does it work? Dixons' story

UK electrical retailer Dixons Group plc has over 1,100 stores in the UK alone and substantial direct sales operations. In 2003, Dixons halved Card Not Present fraud through the use of security measures such as those described above.

Peter Robinson, Dixons Group retail controller, says that 'The use of the AVS address and CSC card code validation services, while still not guaranteeing payment, do offer a better level of validation than we previously had. This in turn enables us to make quicker, more informed decisions and improve customer service. For web-based orders, we use an array of other tools to verify that the order is genuine and placed by the rightful holder of the card. These range from checking previous order history and the banding of transaction values to trigger different security checks to using a third party to undertake further address checks. Collectively, these help us spot any inconsistencies that might spell fraud.'

Online auctions

It's easy to fall into an 'us and them' mindset, with 'us' as card holders and 'them' as merchants. Today, however, more and more of us are disposing of unwanted goods on online auction services such as eBay or Yahoo!Auctions. When selling online, of course, we become the merchants, and are ourselves vulnerable to Card Not Present fraud.

🔓 Beth's story

Beth sells orchids and other garden products on eBay. In 2003 she made a small sale for $15, received payment through the PayPal electronic payments service and dispatched the item. The first indication she had that she was a victim came when she received an email from PayPal stating: 'We regret to inform you that you received funds from an account with reports of fraudulent bank account use. In accordance with PayPal's Seller Protection Policy, the following transaction involving unauthorised funds has been reversed.' In other words, the buyer had committed Card Not Present fraud and Beth had been subject to a charge back.

While Beth was unlucky, at least the cost was small. eBay sellers offering expensive items such as laptop computers often report receiving emails from buyers offering full price, or even more, for the goods and requesting shipping to destinations such as Romania or Indonesia, while offering to pay by credit card.

Often, once the payment is received and the goods have been shipped, the card will turn out to have been stolen or used fraudulently, and the money will be clawed back from the unfortunate seller.

Advice site UKAuctionHelp.co.uk says: 'While it seems unfair to tarnish whole countries, Indonesia, Romania and some other ex-Soviet Republics appear to be a hot bed of credit card fraud, so be very wary of Indonesian transactions by credit card, either directly or via PayPal, etc.'

Chapter 6

The Treasure in your Trash

In the previous chapter we discussed discarded receipts as a source of credit and debit card information. In this chapter I shall look at what else we throw away and the ways in which we put ourselves at risk from identity theft by doing so.

🔓 Drugs and dumpsters

In 2000, identity thieves Stephen Massey and Kari Melton were sentenced to 41 and 15 months respectively in federal jail. Prosecutors claimed they had stolen hundreds of thousands of dollars, although Melton believes the true figure was over $1 million.

Although Massey was a former businessman and Melton was a computer expert there was nothing hi-tech about their methods. It all started when Massey, who had become addicted to the stimulant drug methamphetemine, was invited by fellow addicts to visit the local dump, in a search for saleable items.

'It was the first time I had ever been to the dump,' Massey told an interviewer from the New York Times. 'I said, "I'm not going to get dirty," so I wandered over to a shed where the recycling was stored. I notice there's a big barrel for recycled paper that's full of discarded tax forms from an accounting firm.' Each form had the person's name, date of birth, Social Security number – all the information necessary for taking out a line of credit.

Spotting the potential, Massey instructed his fellow addicts to load up the paperwork and his new career as an identity thief had begun. With the information gathered from the dump Massey would visit the websites of credit companies and apply for cards in his victims' names. He would use a victim's true address to pass the credit scoring process, but then claim to have moved house to a new address, which was a temporary mail drop he had rented for the purpose. In another twist he would ask for a second card, made out in his own name, allowing him to use his own ID when needed.

When Massey met Melton the scheme became more sophisticated. Having put together the information obtained on a person they would then order a credit report online at a cost of a few dollars, seeking to establish the victim's worth, and in particular whether they were a home owner.

'I would know what I'm dealing with before I'd invest time in the person's Social Security number,' Melton said. 'If you have the credit to get a home loan, you have the credit I need.'

In addition to using mail drops, Massey and Melton purchased a number of pre-paid mobile phones to answer queries from the credit card companies. At one time Massey claimed to have had 15 different phones active, each with a note attached identifying the victim to be impersonated should it ring.

Eventually the duo were running a gang of drug addicts who performed the routine work of the operation, raiding trash, sorting papers and transcribing details. By the time they were caught Massey and Melton had left a trail of fraud that was almost impossible to unravel. They were travelling back and forth from their base in Oregon to Las Vegas, where a $1,000 cash advance on a credit card raises no eyebrows, all on other peoples identities. They were only caught when one of Massey's subordinates, being chased by a security guard for breaking into a car, ran to Massey's hotel room, leading the police straight to him.

Although there is a great deal of media coverage concerning the risks to individuals of online identity theft (and such risks do exist, as we'll see in chapter 9), one of the identity thieves' favourite targets is still old-fashioned discarded paper. The process of searching through trash for useful documents is known as 'dumpster diving' in the United States and 'bin raiding' in the UK. Typically the identity thief will use people lower down the criminal ladder to do the actual digging through the trash. Sources suggest that the going rate for recovered documents is at least £5 per document in London and $5 in the US. An employee of Camden council described in the London *Evening Standard* the case of one recently caught bin raider, who said that the amount he was paid varied according to the value of the documents he recovered: 'He told us that whenever he got something with a name and address on it he would be paid a fiver and that something with card numbers or bank details could be worth as much as £50.'

There are three main targets for the dumpster diver:

1 Household rubbish;
2 Business rubbish;
3 The municipal dump or recycling centre.

They are looking for any documents or information they can use to steal an identity: bankcard numbers and receipts, bank statements, utility bills, any official letters, credit card offers, other financial and personal documents, employment or tax records, etc. The current obsession with recycling paper gives them much greater opportunities.

The August 2000 edition of the *FBI Law Enforcement Bulletin* describes a dumpster diver who would drive around affluent neighbourhoods on garbage collection day, picking up garbage bags left at the curb. On taking them home he would look for Social Security numbers and pre-approved credit cards, using a rented mailbox to hide his identity and location. The article notes: 'Many taxpayers dispose of old receipts and financial records carelessly. By encouraging people to shred documents and by enforcing local trespass ordinances with regard to residential and industrial dump sites, law enforcement agencies can prevent thousands of identity theft cases.'

Household rubbish

Despite warnings in the media, pickings in household rubbish are rich. In 2002 credit reference firm Experian conducted a survey in which they examined the contents of 400 household rubbish bins in Nottingham, England. The results were shocking:

- Only 14 per cent of household rubbish bins contained no information of interest to fraudsters;
- On average, one in five bins contained a full credit or debit card number, most with the expiry date. In more affluent areas the figure was two in five;
- One in five bins contained a bank account number and sort code that could be linked to an individual's full name and address. Again the figure was higher among well-off single professionals;
- One in six bins contained a utility bill and one in four contained other official letters;
- One bin contained a signed, blank cheque, while another contained a whole unused chequebook.

Perhaps the most dramatic example, however, was the bin containing the following information and documents, all relating to the same individual:

- Full name and address;
- Date of birth;
- Bank account number and sort code;
- Employment details;
- Medical information;
- Benefit book;
- Utility bill;
- Other official letters;
- Completed passport application.

In other words, an individual's entire life was there in the trash waiting to be found! The report concluded:

It is clear from our research that the risk of bin raiding represents a clear danger to consumers, providing proven opportunities for both credit transaction fraud and identity theft. Bin raiders looking for credit card receipts currently enjoy an average one in five chance of success. In more affluent areas, which is probably where bin raiders would target, this success rate is increased to two in every five bins.

For more sophisticated fraudsters, who might be looking to commit 'account take-over' fraud, the opportunity for success occurs at an average rate of one in six bins. In more affluent areas, the chance of success can be increased to around one in four bins.

ID theft can even happen to Feds

Around 2002, federal government employee Julia Ray received a demand from the IRS for unpaid taxes. Surprised she called the IRS to explain that her taxes were all in order and she didn't believe she owed any money. After a brief discussion about her employment the IRS officer said, 'Oh, it's not for that job. It's for your other job washing dishes.'

A brief investigation discovered that an identity thief had used Julia's Social Security number to gain employment in another state. All he'd done was conceal the fact that they were of opposite sexes by changing 'Julia' to 'Julio'.

To this day Julia has no idea how the criminal got her SSN. 'I can only assume it was on something I threw in the trash,' she said. 'I'll definitely be more careful with what I throw out in future.'

Business rubbish

In November 2003, following the study above, Experian again analysed rubbish, this time from 71 business premises in London. They found that the majority of businesses surveyed were throwing out 'personal and financial information on their clients, individual customers and employees with little or no attempt to shred or properly destroy personal data.' The following list highlights some of the finds:

- A PR agency discarded confidential client PR strategies and embargoed press releases;
- A theatrical agent discarded the names and addresses and mobile phone numbers of well-known film and TV stars;
- A travel agent discarded photocopies of passports with passport numbers, dates of birth, photos, etc;
- An educational establishment discarded financial details of course applicants;
- An architect discarded full detailed plans of NHS hospitals;
- A surgery discarded full medical records of its patients;
- A barristers' chambers discarded signed affidavits and witness statements;
- A mortgage broker discarded numerous completed mortgage applications containing full financial details of its clients.

Other items thrown away by companies included:

- Employees' payslips, including name and National Insurance numbers;

- A Bankers' Automated Clearing System authorised user number;
- Tax schedules, including name, address, date of birth, marital status, NI number, tax reference, residency details, bank details and wage details of employees;
- Bank account details and full profiles of customers;
- Blank company headed paper.

Clearly business rubbish provides very rich pickings for identity thieves.

Is it a crime?

Sadly the legal situation here is murky to say the least. While fraudulent use of documents taken from rubbish is clearly a crime it is not as clear whether the act of taking them breaches the law.

In England and Wales, the question would appear to be one of whether or not the rubbish is abandoned property. The issue of control is quite important here. For example, rubbish deposited in council refuse bins becomes the property of the council. Similarly one might conclude that a privately owned skip on premises owned and secured by a company would be deemed to be in that company's control and therefore that taking it would be theft.

The UK's most famous bin diver is probably a man named Benjamin Pell, aka 'Benjie the Binman', although I wish to make absolutely clear that his motivation is not identity theft. The BBC reports that Mr Pell has been convicted for stealing rubbish from law firms and 'regularly fishes for stories among the rubbish of celebrities and politicians'.

In the US however the 1988 case of California vs Greenwood in the Supreme Court paints a different picture.

🔓 California vs Greenwood

Acting on information indicating that respondent Greenwood might be engaged in narcotics trafficking, police twice obtained from his regular trash collector garbage bags that he had left on the curb in front of his house. On the basis of items in the bags that were indicative of narcotics use, the police obtained warrants to search the house, discovered controlled substances during the searches, and arrested respondents on felony narcotics charges.

The state Superior Court dismissed the charges on the grounds that probable cause to search the house would not have existed without the evidence obtained from the trash searches and that warrantless trash searches violate the Fourth Amendment. The prosecution appealed.

The Supreme Court held, in part, that the Fourth Amendment does not prohibit the warrantless search and seizure of garbage left for collection outside the curtilage of a home since the 'respondents voluntarily left their trash for collection in an area particularly suited for public inspection,' therefore 'their claimed expectation of privacy in the inculpatory items they discarded was not objectively reasonable.'

The court went on to say 'It is common knowledge that plastic garbage bags left along a public street are readily accessible to animals, children, scavengers, snoops, and other members of the public.'

🔓 The dumpster diver's story

In late 2000 a woman calling herself Lana posted an account of her dumpster diving career and eventual arrest behind a Fortune 100 company to a hacker website.

Lana began by practising her trash raiding on her neighbours. Sneaking out at night she would grab a couple of bags of trash and take them back to her garage to investigate her haul. Describing the contents she said:

'It is truly amazing what people will throw away without shredding first. I now know my neighbour's credit card, checking account, and Social Security numbers, as well as what medications they are taking.'

Disdaining the opportunities for identity theft provided by her neighbours' carelessness as 'tempting maybe, but not a good idea', Lana moved up a level, targeting her first local retailer. It was at this stage that her operation began to become more sophisticated. Her modus operandi was as follows:

- 🔒 Begin by observing the rear of the store at night;
- 🔒 Note delivery and garbage collection times;
- 🔒 Repeat over seven days to determine any patterns;
- 🔒 Dress smartly to lend plausibility to any story in the event of being caught.

'My first mission was a success. I was able to get some user IDs and passwords, along with a company phone book,' Lana wrote.

After another raid, in which she describes being caught by a policeman and successfully obtaining his assistance in searching for her 'lost engagement ring', Lana turned her attentions to a big company and was caught. This time her story was not believed, and she was asked to sign a form promising not to trespass on that company's property again. This was hardly a deterrent:

'Since I am not an idiot, I realise the system is working in my favour. To beat the system, I just move from one company to another,' she writes. 'You won't be charged and will get tons of great information. Goodbye jail time, hello companies!'

How to protect yourself

There are a number of different areas of exposure, and while we can have a great deal of control over some of them, such as our own trash, we have a lot less control over our employer or the companies we do business with. Even so, we can minimise our risk:

1   Take care of your identity, personal information, transaction slips and proofs of identity by keeping your documents secure.

2   Never throw away whole receipts, bank statements, utility bills and other documents that can be used by a fraudster to assume your identity, or compromise your credit/banking facilities. Your refuse is a target for fraudsters. Always thoroughly destroy personal information before throwing in the bin, preferably with a personal shredder; small ones can be bought from most stationary shops. Lana, our dumpster diver, has this advice: 'Above all, protect yourself at home! Shred everything, no matter how trivial the items may seem. You are very naïve if you think someone is not sifting through your garbage looking for valuable information.'

3 If you can't shred them then try to dispose of torn-up documents containing personal or financial information in separate bins, eg half at home and half at work.

4 Never put personal documents into a recycling bin.

5 Ask your employer what procedures they have for disposing of sensitive documents such as payroll and tax information.

6 Ask the companies you do business with what their policies are. Remember, in Europe companies processing personal data have a duty of care to protect their customers' information under Data Protection legislation. In the US there are laws, such as Chapter 19.215 RCW Disposal of Personal Information, in Washington State, which holds in part that companies 'must take all reasonable steps to destroy, or arrange for the destruction of, personal financial and health information and personal identification numbers issued by government entities in an individual's records within its custody or control when the entity is disposing of records that it will no longer retain.'

Poetic justice

With four arrests for drunk driving to his name, Florida resident James Perry rightly felt that he'd have trouble getting a driver's licence. But he felt that he really needed one, so eventually he raided the trash in his next-door neighbour's yard.

The raid went well and when Perry moved to Connecticut a year later he was able to parlay the stolen documents into a Connecticut driver's licence in the name of his former neighbour, Raymond Kowalski.

All went well for around another year until late 2003 when, during an alleged domestic dispute, Perry's then girlfriend called 911, the police emergency number. Arriving at the scene, police arrested Perry – who gave his name as Raymond Kowalski – for disorderly conduct.

That's when the bottom fell out of James Perry's world. Upon running a routine computer background check the police found that their suspect, who they still believed to be Kowalski, was a convicted sex offender in Michigan, and was not registered with the state of Connecticut as the law required.

Although Perry was adamant that he was no sex offender every piece of ID in his possession gave his name as Kowalski. Eventually an FBI fingerprint check proved he was Perry. He was then promptly charged with identity theft and forgery.

Chapter 7
Social Engineering

In April 2004 the organisers of Infosecurity Europe, an information security conference, conducted an impromptu survey at a major London commuter railway station. Seventy-one per cent of the office workers surveyed were willing to give away their passwords in exchange for a chocolate bar.

I sincerely wish that I could tell you that the above statement was a joke. Sadly it's not. Rather it is a rather crude example of a technique known as 'social engineering', a con trick whereby fraudsters get us to divulge our personal information or secrets, often without us realising that we've done so.

The pretext call

Pretext calling is an old, established technique where the caller pretends to be somebody in order to gain access to information that would not otherwise be revealed. As well as being used by identity thieves the technique has also been popular with private investigators, people compiling lists of sales prospects and even law enforcement agencies investigating specific crimes.

Pretext calls to individuals

Identity thieves using the pretext call to steal your identity directly will usually use one of a few tried and tested tactics. They may pretend to be from your bank or credit card company, to be from a market research company conducting a survey, or to be from a company or organisation you do business with.

⌔ The Scottish connection

In March 2004 Dumfries and Galloway police issued the following warning to residents.

A woman from the Dumfries area received a telephone call from a man who said that he was from her bank and was advising her that someone else was trying to use her bankcard. The woman checked and found that her purse, with the card, had been stolen.

The caller, who was said to be well spoken, reassured the woman by giving her name and address which, of course, he had obtained from her stolen purse. Because she believed that the caller was from the bank, she gave him her PIN number, which he said he needed to stop any transactions on her account. It was only when she checked her accounts later that she found that almost the instant she gave her PIN number, several hundred pounds had been withdrawn.

Pretext callers always give a seemingly valid reason for contacting you. If pretending to be calling from a financial institution they may say that there have been problems with your account or that they have found suspected fraudulent activity. Fake market researchers will run through a plausible survey establishing whatever they can about your financial particulars and personal information. They may even try to establish when your property will be unoccupied, in order to burgle it. Those claiming to be from organisations you do business with may claim to be chasing an unpaid bill or to be calling with a special offer. Other tactics include pretending to be from your Internet Service Provider or even the police or the government.

One of the more successful approaches involves the fraudster calling their victims in the evening, outside office hours, claiming to be from a utility company. The thief will claim that due to a mix up there is an outstanding water, gas or electricity bill and, unless payment is made immediately by credit card, the supply of the utility in question will be disconnected that night.

How to protect yourself

Quite simply, don't give out personal information to anybody unless you know who you are dealing with. Ideally you should have initiated the contact. Be especially wary of anybody who cold calls you. Ask them which organisation they're calling from and, if appropriate, call them back on a telephone number you know to be accurate, such as the number printed on the back of your credit card or on a utility bill. Never call back on a number they give you. Also, be wary whenever anybody claiming to be from your financial institution asks for a complete PIN or password. Most banks will only ask for certain, randomly selected, digits or characters.

 ## Robin's story

I was off work, sick, one day. At around 11 am the phone rang. I answered it and the man said he was calling from my bank, about some suspicious transactions on one of my cards. I'd had a card cloned before so I guessed this was what was up. Our conversation went something like this:

Me: Oh dear, are you saying it's been cloned again?
Him: Well sir, I'm afraid I can't reveal any information until I've confirmed your identity with some security questions.
Me: Well, with respect I don't know who you are. How about if I call the number on the back of my card and ask them to put me through to you?
Him: That's a very sensible security precaution, sir.

After phoning my bank myself and going through the security procedures I found out the call had been genuine. But it left me wondering, if it's so sensible to call the bank myself, why didn't he ask me to do that in the first place? Especially as my bank's website says, 'Always be wary of unsolicited calls or emails requesting you to disclose your personal security information.'

Pretext calls to banks

Identity thieves don't just limit themselves to calling individuals. Often banks are the target. Furnished with a few pieces of personal information, such as a name, address, card or account number and so forth, the identity thief will pretext call the bank, pretending to be the customer. The thief may just want further financial information. Alternatively he may try to submit a change of address as part of a scheme to obtain statements, which are useful as ID for opening new accounts or even to obtain a new credit card or cheque book.

How to protect yourself

As is often the case when we're dealing with another organisation's security protocols, rather than our own, there is a limit to what we can do. Assuming we're careful not to divulge our information the next step is to agree strong passwords and security phrases with our bank.

Never use your mother's maiden name as a security word. This point can't be made too often or emphasised too strongly. Your mother's maiden name is a matter of public record. Even if the bank insists, make something up and use that instead.

What banks can do

Banking, like most businesses these days, tries (with greater or lesser success) to be a customer-service oriented business. Pretext callers take advantage of the fact that banks don't want to put too many hurdles in the way of their legitimate customers.

That said, banks should and do take steps to defend against pretext calling. The Office of the Comptroller of the

Currency (part of the United States Department of the Treasury) gives the following guidelines to banks.

1. Limiting telephone disclosures

There are a number of ways in which banks may limit access to customer information. One way is to permit employees to release information over the telephone only if the individual requesting the information provides a proper authorisation code. The code should be different than other commonly used numbers or identifiers, such as Social Security numbers, savings, checking, loan, or other financial account numbers, or the maiden name of the customer's mother. The authorisation code should be unique to, and capable of being changed readily by, the authorised account holder. To be most effective, the authorisation code should be used in conjunction with other customer and account identifiers.

Another means of preventing unauthorised disclosures of customer information is to use a caller identification system (ie CallerID™). If the telephone number displayed differs from that in the customer's account records, it may be an indication that the request is not legitimate and the employee should not disclose the requested account information without taking additional steps to verify that the true customer is making the request. In the absence of a caller identification system, banks could require employees who receive calls for account information to ask the caller for the number from which he or she is calling or for a call-back number. If the individual refuses to provide the number or it doesn't match the information in the customer's records, the employee should not disclose the information without additional measures to verify that the caller is the true customer.

2. Employee training

Banks should train staff to recognise unauthorised or fraudulent attempts to obtain customer information. In addition to an employee's inability to match a caller's telephone number with that on file, there may be other indicators of a pretext call. For instance, a caller who cannot provide all relevant information requested, or a caller who is abusive or who tries to distract the employee, may be a pretext caller. Employees should be trained to recognise such devices and, under such circumstances, protect customer information through appropriate measures, such as by taking additional steps to verify that the caller is a bona fide customer.

Employees should be trained to implement the bank's written policies and procedures governing the disclosure of customer information, and should be informed not to deviate from them. Moreover, employees must know to whom and how to report suspicious activity that may be a pretext call. Banks may have a fraud department or contact to whom the employee reports suspicious activities, or may establish another means for reporting possible fraud. Known or suspected federal criminal violations should be reported to law enforcement in accordance with the procedures discussed below.

3. Testing

Banks should test the key controls and procedures of their information security systems and consider using independent staff or third parties to conduct unscheduled pretext phone calls to various departments to evaluate the institution's susceptibility to unauthorised disclosures of customer information. Any weaknesses should be addressed through enhanced training, procedures, or controls, or a combination of these elements.

🔓 Red faces in the UK

In December 2003, after yet another 'phishing attack' (a scam where crooks send an email pretending to be from your bank in order to con you into revealing your card details) targeted customers of Lloyds TSB, a high street bank in the UK, the bank said, 'We are very confident about the security of our internet banking site – and it is our top priority – **but customers must ensure they keep their security details secret**.'

In March 2004, customers of Lloyds TSB reported receiving a text message on their phone saying, 'Please call Lloyds TSB on 0870 xxx xxxx.' Customers who called the number were promptly asked for their name and credit card number.

A spokesman for Lloyds TSB admitted that this happened but said that the bank only used this technique to contact customers who were in arrears and who had failed to respond to other means of contact, such as a letter. 'We would never ask for full account information,' he said, 'only partial information sufficient to confirm the customer's identity.' The spokesman went on to say that the customers contacted in this manner would know that they were in arrears and would therefore be expecting to be contacted. 'This method of making contact is never used for any other purposes such as marketing,' he concluded.

Unfortunately this misses the point. What if the next text message the customer received asking them to call the bank actually came from a criminal? Security is a partnership between financial institutions and their customers. In my opinion activities such as this run the risk of breeding an environment of carelessness, which could make disclosure of personal information to identity thieves more likely. Betsy Broeder of the US Federal Trade Commission says, 'Only divulge personal information if you initiated the exchange or you know who you're dealing with.' No text message from a bank should ever say more than something along the lines of: 'Please call [name of bank] on the telephone number printed on the back of your card.'

Fake documents

This scam is similar to the pretext call attack except instead of telephoning the thief will write to you, using a fake letterhead purporting to be from your bank, your accountant, the government or some other trusted party.

The most common example currently circulating uses fictitious bank correspondence and US Internal Revenue Service (IRS) forms in an attempt to trick taxpayers into disclosing their personal and banking data. The information fraudulently obtained is then used to steal the taxpayer's identity and bank account deposits.

The scam has been spotted coast-to-coast throughout the US, including in Maine, New York, Georgia, North Carolina, Texas, California and the state of Washington. Dozens of US and foreign victims have been identified so far. More recently, warnings have been issued that the scam is spreading to Europe and the IRS has asked banks to alert their overseas branches so that they may warn their customers.

In this scam, a letter claiming to be from the taxpayer's bank states that the 'bank' is updating its records in order to exempt the taxpayer from reporting interest or having tax withheld on interest paid on his or her bank accounts or other financial dealings.

The correspondence encloses a phoney form that purports to come from the IRS and seeks detailed personal and financial data. The letter urges the recipient to fax the completed form to a specific number within seven days or lose the reporting and withholding exemption, resulting in withholding of 31 per cent on the account's interest. The scheme promoters then use the faxed information to impersonate the taxpayer and gain access to the taxpayer's finances.

One such phoney form is labelled 'W-9095, Application Form for Certificate Status/Ownership for Withholding Tax'. The form requests personal data frequently used to prove identity, including passport number and mother's maiden name. It also asks for sensitive financial data such as bank account numbers, passwords and PIN numbers that can be used to gain access to the accounts.

The fictitious W-9095 appears to be an attempt to mimic the genuine IRS Form W-9, 'Request for Taxpayer Identification Number and Certification'. The only personal information a genuine W-9 requests is the name, address and Social Security number or employer identification number of the taxpayer.

A variation on the scam targets citizens of other countries who have dealings with the United States or who bank there. Here the fake form used in the scam is Form W-8BEN, 'Certificate of Foreign Status of Beneficial Owner for United States Tax Withholding'. There is a legitimate IRS Form W-8BEN, which is used by banks to ensure that their non-US customers meet the criteria to remain exempt from tax reporting requirements. However, the W-8BEN used by the scam promoters has been altered to ask for personal information much like the W-9095.

Another totally fictitious IRS form used in this scam is labelled 'W-8888'. It too asks for information similar to the phoney W-9095 and W-8BEN.

How to protect yourself

Treat any unsolicited letters asking for personal information just as you'd treat a cold call. Verify them with your bank or whichever organisation they purport to come from. Look closely at the address you're being asked to return the information to and verify that with a publicly available source. Don't give your valuable private information away.

The bogus job offer

🔓 Preying on the vulnerable

In 2002 Joe, an unemployed manager with 20 years experience, was looking for a job. Days after replying to an advert for a senior position with a multinational company, Joe was delighted to hear that he'd got the job, subject to successfully completing a background check. As a former Navy officer Joe had no concerns about passing the check and promptly filled in and returned the form.

When he didn't hear anything further Joe called the company's human resources director, whose phone number was on the letter he'd received. The line was disconnected.

Joe had fallen for one of the cruellest social engineering attacks currently in play. And the fraudsters now had all the information they needed to steal his identity.

Most of us know the difficulties of looking for a job. As people get older it can become even harder to find work, leading them to feel desperate. Desperation is what the fraudsters prey on.

They take out adverts, in newspapers or on online job sites. Often they will impersonate large, successful or well-known companies. Everybody who applies is told that they've got the job, or have been shortlisted for it at least, subject to completing a background check.

Of course the 'background check' is nothing of the sort. It's simply a way for them to plausibly ask you to provide all the personal information they need to steal your identity.

A new twist – money laundering

In a variation on the scam, organised criminals are recruiting people to act as unwitting money launderers. Gangsters recruit job seekers to act as 'payment processors' or 'correspondence managers' then route dirty money (sometimes taken directly from the accounts of other identity theft victims) through their accounts. The victims are promised a percentage but are left with a bill. In other cases recruits are asked to forward packages. One victim forwarded 750 packages with an average value of $1,500 to Russia, according to the United States Postal Inspection Service (USPIS).

How to protect yourself

Many of the major online job sites, such as Monster.com, CareerBuilder.com and HotJobs.com post warnings on their sites. Broadly speaking you should be aware that while it is normal for a prospective employer to want to know your contact details, work experience, education, previous employers, etc, it is most certainly not normal for them to ask for your credit card details, tax information, Social Security number or National Insurance number, bank account number, date of birth and so on. Sure, the payroll or accounts department will need some of this information in order to pay you, but not until you're employed by the company.

1   Do not give out your credit card or bank numbers;

2   Never engage in any financial transactions with a prospective employer;

3   Do not give out any non-essential personal information (eg Social Security number, NI number, eye colour, marital status, etc) over the phone or online;

4   Do not give out this information, even if they suggest that it is for a 'routine background check';

5   Be cautious when dealing with contacts outside your own country;

6   When approached by somebody claiming to be from a company ask for their contact information, and then independently look up the company's phone number and call them to verify that the company is legitimate and the person who approached you actually works there in a legitimate capacity;

7 Be cautious of prospective employers who ask you to reply through a third-party address that doesn't bear the company's name or trademark.

There are many other forms of social engineering. The 'helpful stranger' at the ATM, who we encountered earlier in this book, is practising a crude form of social engineering. Other attacks are more cunning. I'll give two more examples below, but the key fact is that no matter how plausible an approach might appear, the only sensible course of action is to be suspicious of anybody who asks for your personal information.

The newspaper advert

This scam is a variant on the standard pretext call but operates in reverse. The thieves place advertisements in local newspapers, apparently from a bank, credit union or other financial institution. The ads will feature the financial institution's logo and branding and provide a plausible reason for their customers to call them. The phone number, of course, is fake.

Those who call are asked to provide personal information that can then be used to obtain credit information and open fraudulent accounts. In some instances, callers are also asked for immediate payment for services supposedly offered by the scammers.

How to protect yourself

This scam works because the victim believes that they are initiating the contact. In fact, you are not, at least not if you call the number in the ad. Whenever you have to deal with your financial institutions always use a telephone number that you know to be accurate.

The phoney identity theft prevention service

Recently a number of companies have started to offer consumers 'identity theft protection services' for a fee. While legitimate insurance policies do exist (although experts are divided as to whether they're worth the money), some of the so-called services are actually scams, operated by fraudsters in order to steal your identity.

The following query is typical of those from people who do decide to check with their bank after receiving such a call:

'I got a call from a woman who said I need credit card loss protection insurance. I thought there was a law that limited my liability to $50 for unauthorised charges. But she said the law had changed and that now, people are liable for all unauthorised charges on their account. Is that true?'

♪ The crooks robbed those they were paid to protect

In September 202 Philip Arcand and Roberta Galway were indicted by a federal grand jury in Birmingham, Alabama on 158 counts of telemarketing fraud, bank fraud, money laundering and other crimes.

According to the charges the two set up companies registered in the UK, US, British Virgin Isles and Nicaragua, then began selling phoney credit card protection schemes by telephone to elderly credit card holders in the United States at up to $299 a time. They then used the credit card accounts that they were supposed to be protecting to steal money, which they laundered through their network of companies and through fraudulently opened bank accounts. The indictment alleged that the defendants netted $3 million through selling the phoney protection scheme and that Arcand netted another $9.4 million through fraudulent charges.

The pair had already been ordered to pay $436,000 in a case brought by the Federal Trade Commission (FTC) for the deceptive telesales charges. In 2003, Arcand was sentences by the court in Alabama to 39 months in prison and ordered to pay restitution of $4,298,385.10.

How to protect yourself

The FTC gives the following advice, under the heading 'Credit Card Loss Protection Offers: They're the Real Steal'.

Don't buy the pitch – and don't buy the 'loss protection' insurance. Telephone scam artists are lying to get people to buy worthless credit card loss protection and insurance programs. If you didn't authorize a charge, don't pay it. Follow your credit card issuer's procedures for disputing charges you haven't authorized. According to the Federal Trade Commission, your liability for unauthorized charges is limited to $50.

The FTC says worthless credit card loss protection offers are popular among fraudulent promoters who are trying to exploit consumers' uncertainty. As a result, the agency is cautioning consumers to avoid doing business with callers who claim that:

🔒 You're liable for more than $50 in unauthorised charges on your credit card account [this is £50 in the UK but it is usually waived];

🔒 You need credit card loss protection because computer hackers can access your credit card number and charge thousands of dollars to your account;

🔒 A computer bug could make it easy for thieves to place unauthorised charges on your credit card account; and

🔒 They're from 'the security department' and want to activate the protection feature on your credit card.

The FTC advises consumers not to give out personal information – including their credit card or bank account numbers – over the phone or online unless they are familiar with the business that's asking for it.

The law

Again, law in the US is ahead of the UK. In the US the 1999 Financial Modernisation Act (AKA the Gramm-Leach-Bliley Act) makes it illegal under federal law for anyone to:

🔒 Use false, fictitious or fraudulent statements or documents to get customer information from a financial institution or directly from a customer of a financial institution.

🔒 Use forged, counterfeit, lost or stolen documents to get customer information from a financial institution or directly from a customer of a financial institution.

🔒 Ask another person to get someone else's customer information using false, fictitious or fraudulent statements or using false, fictitious or fraudulent documents or forged, counterfeit, lost, or stolen documents.

In the UK the law is framed in terms of data protection. Under the Data Protection Act 1998, it is an offence for a person 'knowingly or recklessly, without the consent of the data controller, to obtain personal data. If a person has obtained information in contravention of the Act, it is an offence to sell or offer to sell that data.'

In practice, however, enforcement in this area seems to be targeted more at private investigators and debt collection agencies. In September 2002, Alistair Fraser, trading as Solent Credit Control in Portsmouth, pleaded guilty to offences of unlawfully obtaining and selling personal information in breach of the Data Protection Act 1998. He asked for 66 similar offences to be taken into consideration. Fraser was fined £1,400 in total and ordered to pay £1,000 costs.

The prosecution was brought by the Information Commissioner as a result of a joint investigation initiative between the Information Commissioner, the Inland Revenue and the Department for Work and Pensions. The investigation was initiated as a direct result of the Inland Revenue recognising that it was regularly being targeted by tracing agencies trying to obtain information.

This investigation has clearly had an impact in some areas – one private investigator said 'I used to boast that I could trace 70 per cent of debtors. Now the figure is much more like 50 per cent.' Whether this will have any impact on identity theft remains to be seen.

Chapter 8

Giving it all Away

Whereas with social engineering we are duped into disclosing information, it is easy to simply give away information at any time due to poor management of our personal life, or rather carelessness.

Identity thieves make it their business to be informed about things we ordinarily wouldn't think of. It's only by taking care to ensure that we are as informed as they that we can defeat their attempts. Often that means identifying and closing security holes in various aspects of our lives. These security holes are things that would never occur to most of us, but which the identity thieves are on the look out for.

Telephones and PINs

Mobile phones, answering machines and voicemail are things we all take for granted. But how many of us bother to change the PIN that came with our voicemail account, or even know that it has a PIN? In fact most voicemail systems, including those on mobile phones, are set up to allow the owner of the telephone to retrieve messages remotely; that is, from a different telephone.

There are two common systems. Sometimes the owner calls their own phone number and waits for the voicemail to kick in, other times they call a central voicemail number and then enter their own phone number. In either case the next step involves entering a PIN – and almost all phones have a default PIN.

Susan's story

San Francisco businesswoman Susan Steele got a shock when her telephone bill arrived. The phone company wanted more than $20,000 for almost 100 hours of overseas calls, many of them to Saudi Arabia and the Philippines. Susan hadn't made those calls. When she called her own number and listened to her outgoing message it had changed. Instead of her voice she heard something very strange.

'There was this guy answering my phone saying, "Investment company, please hold," then the person would come on and I heard, "Yes, yes, yes,"' Susan said.

Crooks had cracked into Susan's mailbox by guessing the PIN and changed the outgoing message. Later, they began to place international calls via the operator, asking for the charges to be billed to Susan's number. When the operator called the number to confirm that the bill payer was willing to accept the charges, the recorded message simulated a person agreeing to accept them, and so the calls were put through.

Susan's PIN '1234', was easily guessed. As I said above, most voicemail accounts have a default PIN, and many customers never bother to change it. Criminals circulate the PINs among themselves and in any case they are easy to track down on the internet.

How to protect yourself

Access all your voicemail devices, answering machines, etc now and change the PIN. Don't pick a PIN that is easy to guess and don't use the default PIN. Check your voicemail every so often to make sure that it still plays your outgoing message. Finally remember it's not just your mobile phone that's vulnerable. Many company telephone exchanges allow call forwarding and direct dial. If your voicemail box at work has a vulnerable PIN you could have some explaining to do.

Don't forget your mail

Mail theft is a problem on both sides of the Atlantic and although arrangements for domestic mail in the US are in many ways different from those in the UK there are some similarities as well as differences in the patterns of the crime.

According to APACS 'mail non-receipt fraud' accounted for 9 per cent of the cost of card fraud in the UK in 2002. In the US the FTC found that 8 per cent of identity theft victims who said that they knew how their personal information was obtained by the thief cited stolen mail as the source of the information.

Likewise, the chances of having your mail stolen increase with the quantity of mail. Authorities in both countries advise taking steps to have a hold put on your mail while on holiday.

The differences largely tend to be in the manner in which the mail is stolen. In the US the prevalence of publicly accessible mail boxes outside houses and in communal areas of apartment blocks has led to organised gangs of mail thieves who use your mail as the first link in their chain of identity theft crimes.

In the UK, mail theft tends to be the work of insiders employed at the Royal Mail or opportunists who take advantage of mis-delivered post, mail in a communal area or simply pick it up as part of a burglary.

🔒 An organised network

In September 2003, Igor Kogan, Mikhail Moiseev and a number of other men were sentenced in federal court in San Francisco for a number of felonies related to identity theft. Other members of their network were already in jail and more were awaiting trial. Prosecutors had taken down an identity theft network worth more than $1 million a year.

Although resident in San Francisco, Kogan along with his accomplice Moiseev would drive out to the affluent Bay Area to begin operations. With one of them keeping watch the other would rifle through mailboxes by the side of the road. Their target: pre-approved credit cards. Once they had the cards it was back to the big city, where accomplices would use the cards for the usual high-value purchases favoured by identity thieves. Prosecutors estimated that the gang stole and used more than 800 credit cards belonging to victims in the Bay Area.

Kogan received two 13-month sentences for conspiracy, theft of mail, aiding and abetting and unauthorised use of an access device. He was told he would be under supervision for three years upon his release and was ordered to pay $50,000 restitution. Moiseev was given ten months jail, with three years supervised release, for unauthorised use of an access device and aiding and abetting. He was ordered to pay $8,000 restitution.

❧ An inside job

In May 2002 Austin Pius, a 30-year-old postman, was sentenced to two years and three months imprisonment at Inner London Crown Court for stealing mail comprising identity documents, utility bills, cheques and credit cards. When he was caught by police he had been employed by the Royal Mail for only a few days.

At a later Confiscation Hearing, His Honour Judge Stone heard evidence that, in addition to using the stolen credit cards, Pius had fraudulently operated bank accounts and passed stolen cheques through these accounts. Benefit from his criminal conduct was determined to be £147,752 plus $700. A Confiscation Order was made in the sum of realisable assets of £49,757.

When we read about stolen mail leading to identity theft in the UK there's usually a corrupt postal worker involved somewhere. While it is true that theft from within the system plays a major part in underpinning identity theft in the UK it is far from being the only factor. Before we look at the inside job, let's look at the part of the problem that's our fault, the part that's rooted in carelessness.

Who knows where you live?

'I know where you live' has passed into the popular vernacular as an, often humorous, veiled threat. But we want some organisations to know where we live, our banks, employers and so on. According to Experian, areas inhabited by young professionals generated the most post containing sensitive information: 24 per cent of their post. This figure dipped to 14 per cent in 'wealthy family' areas, 7 per cent in 'blue collar' areas and 4 to 5 per cent in council house areas. As well as making good use of credit and store card facilities, young professionals tend to congregate in rental and 'starter home' areas. These properties often have communal areas, making access to mail easier for fraudsters.

According to the Royal Mail figures for 2003, incorrect addressing resulted in 193 million letters being delivered to an address where the recipient had 'gone away'. A large proportion of these letters contained enough information to permit identity fraud.

Risks within the Royal Mail

As the UK's biggest carrier of mail, naturally the Royal Mail endeavours to give a reliable, honest service. When asked to comment on allegations that organised criminals gained employment with the Royal Mail to enable criminal activity a spokeswoman said, 'Incidents of theft by Royal Mail postal workers are extremely rare and the vast majority of our postmen and women are honest and hardworking. Royal Mail takes the security of customers' mail very seriously, and has a team dedicated to ensuring stringent security procedures are deployed across the business. We operate a zero tolerance policy towards the mistreatment of mail in our care.'

In May 2004, testifying before the House of Commons Trade and Industry Committee, Adam Crozier, chief executive of the Royal Mail said, 'The fact is if you employ 200,000 people then, I guess, we have to expect that we will have a few people within that who are, perhaps, not doing what they should be doing,' before going on to explain that the Royal Mail employs 180 dedicated investigators and prosecutors who work hand-in-hand with the police.

Asked about incidences of theft Mr Crozier said, 'What I can tell you is that over the last year as part of our security team's operation we prosecuted around 300 people so we do have a zero tolerance approach to this. Where we find any wrongdoing of that kind we do take action and in fact in certain instances if it is not deemed serious enough by the police we carry on and prosecute on our own basis, which is why we have our own team of prosecutors.'

The Royal Mail denies that any criminal activity is organised on any large scale. However a source close to the investigations branch says that 'criminals do join the Royal Mail for fraud.' While not organised in the traditional sense they are 'organised in the sense of being separate groups with the same contacts, so that two cards stolen from different areas of the country would be found being used in the same place.'

One of the techniques used by criminals is 'the thumb', where a corrupt employee sorting mail will run his or her thumb along an envelope while reading the address. If anything of value is detected, that envelope will be put into the pigeonhole for the employee's own mailbag, allowing him to intercept it at his leisure. Another technique mail investigators look for is systematically delayed mail. Sometimes corrupt staff will take mail home, extract the valuables, and deliver the rest in a day or two.

One thing Mr Crozier and my sources appear to agree upon is the need for better vetting procedures for prospective Royal Mail employees. Mr Crozier told the Committee, 'One of the areas we are looking at is that in certain areas of the business we are allowed to check criminal records. Let's take cash handling in post offices. We are obviously allowed to check people's criminal records but we are not allowed to do that generally across the board, as no company is. We are going to investigate whether it might be possible for the Royal Mail to change that because, in effect, all of our people at times handle valuable objects and that is something we are looking into with the DTI now.'

This would certainly seem to be needed. One source described finding 'villains who were apprehended at one sorting office working again as casual employees at another.' According to this source an old law gave the Royal Mail the right to run background checks on casual employees hired over the Christmas period – but not at any other time of year.

The situation is further confused now that postal services in the UK are open to competition. Royal Mail investigators report having recovered stolen mail only to find that it was never part of a Royal Mail delivery in the first place. In addition, the plethora of carriers simply gives criminals more places to operate. Finally, because there is no central record of individual offences under the Postal Services Act 2000 it is impossible to determine for certain whether the situation is improving or getting worse.

How to protect yourself

Clearly there's a limit to what you can do about what goes on within the postal system. But there's a lot you can do outside it. The United States Postal Inspection Service gives the following advice:

- Promptly remove mail from your mailbox after delivery, especially if you're expecting cheques, credit cards or other valuable items. If you won't be home when the items are expected, ask a trusted friend or neighbour to pick up your mail.

- Have your local post office hold your mail while you're on vacation, or absent from your home for a long period of time.

- If you don't receive a cheque or other valuable mail you're expecting, contact the issuing agency immediately.

- If you change your address, immediately notify your post office and anyone with whom you do business via the mail.

- Always deposit your mail in a mail slot at your local post office, or hand it to your letter carrier.

- Consider starting or joining a neighbourhood watch program. By exchanging work and vacation schedules with trusted friends and neighbours, you can watch each other's mailboxes (as well as homes). If you observe a mail thief at work, call the local police immediately, and then your nearest Postal Inspector.

With the exception of the items referring to outside mail boxes, most of this advice applies to the UK too. The Royal Mail will hold mail for up to two months while you're on holiday or away, for just a small fee. This service is called 'Keepsafe'. Also:

- 🔒 Opt out of receiving credit card offers. Sign up for the mailing preference service if in the UK or contact the three credit reference agencies in the US and have your credit report marked 'no solicitations'.
- 🔒 Once again, make sure everybody you do business with has your current address.

Who's listening?

One of the simplest things we can do to protect against identity theft is to ask ourselves, 'Who's listening, who's watching?' whenever we complete a financial transaction. Identity thieves are always on the lookout for those times when we communicate our personal information to others. Look around before you type in your PIN at an ATM (or soon a retail Point Of Sale terminal). Don't read out your credit card number if there are people within earshot. Fill in forms in private, not in public.

It's hard to believe but I've sat on a bus before now and listened to somebody use his debit card to pay his credit

card bill over his mobile phone. In the course of the transaction he announced the following to anybody within
earshot, his:

- Credit card number;
- Name;
- Date of birth;
- Mother's maiden name;
- First line of his address;
- Debit card number;
- Debit card start and expiry date.

With that information an identity thief could begin running
up charges on his debit card right away, while waiting for a
'replacement' credit card to be sent to a 'new address'.

Apathy

This is simply a catch-all term for a combination of the
mistakes discussed above. In March 2004, UK credit
reference agency Experian published the results of a survey of
UK consumers. According to Experian, the results suggested
that more than 8 million people in the UK would willingly
disclose to an unknown cold caller the exact combination of
personal details a fraudster needs to commit identity fraud,
with men (22 per cent) being far more likely to give out this
information than women (14.5 per cent). Most people wouldn't
even think twice about sharing the two pieces of personal information 'most wanted' by identity thieves: their mother's maiden
name (20 per cent) and their date of birth (46.4 per cent).

Worse, one in seven wouldn't notice if up to £500 disap-
peared from their bank balance and 3.2 per cent could only
estimate to within the nearest £1,000 the survey claimed.

Other findings included the claim that one in ten careless
Brits is at risk from bin raiders: 11.2 per cent admit to simply
throwing financial documents in their bin without shredding or
even ripping them up, putting themselves at serious risk from
'bin-raiding' fraudsters. Less than half (45 per cent) follow
recommended best practice for managing documents, with
many storing documents insecurely.

Chapter 9
Online Identity Theft

For many of us the internet is now a part of everyday life; to others it is still the Wild West, populated by bandits out to rob us and worse. In fact, contrary to popular opinion, most of us are still more at risk of identity theft in real life than we are online. However, the electronic environment does provide a number of opportunities for the identity thieves, some merely computerised versions of traditional scams and others entirely new. Criminals have developed a number of common tactics to steal our identities online, as we shall see.

Phishing

In March 2004, an anonymous reader wrote to his local newspaper, *The San Jose Mercury News,* for help. The unlucky correspondent had given his Social Security number, bank account number and mother's maiden name to a fake PayPal website. 'My information was used to drain my bank account and take $500 of my overdraft protection,' wrote the unlucky victim.

Why would anybody give all that sensitive information to a fake website? The victim above, like many others, fell prey to an online scam called 'phishing'.

'It's been growing tremendously,' says Dan Maier, director of marketing of the Anti-Phishing Working Group. 'The amateurs are starting to get weeded out a bit, but the professional criminals are beginning to take over because what we're seeing is the sophistication level of a lot of the phishing attacks are starting to rise considerably.

'One ISP I was talking to said that they estimate that people who respond to these attacks and give out personal information lost on average about $300 per person. Not quite clear how many people fall for each attack, although we've seen response rates of up to five per cent per phishing attack.'

By April 2004, the monthly volume of phishing emails had risen to 3.1 billion worldwide according to email-filtering firm Brightmail. UK police have estimated that phishing scams cost estimated £60m in the UK alone in 2003. In the US, the economic toll from phishing was nearer $1.2 billion in over the same period, according to Gartner Research.

Phishing is when you receive an email purporting to be from a respectable institution. This could be your bank, an online service provider or even a government agency. In recent years Citibank, Barclays, eBay, PayPal, the United States Federal Government and even the Bank of England have been impersonated.

The emails use a number of different approaches. One in 2003, purporting to be from Barclays, had the subject line 'Security Server Update'. The email went on to say 'Dear valued customer. Our new security system will help you to avoid frequently fraud transactions and to keep your investments in safety,' before inviting recipients to 'reactivate your account' by clicking on a link.

Another, sent in January 2004, purported to come from Citibank:

Dear Citibank Account Holder,

On January 10th 2004 Citibank had to block some accounts in our system connected with money laundering, credit card fraud, terrorism and cheque fraud activity. The information in regards to those accounts has been passed to our correspondent banks, local, federal and international authorities. Due to our extensive database operations some accounts may have been changed. We are asking our customers to check their checking and savings accounts if they are active or if their current balance is correct. Citibank notifies all its customers in cases of high fraud or criminal activity and asks you to check your accounts' balances. If you suspect or have found any fraud activity on your account please let us know by logging in at the link below.

Non-banking examples include an email entitled 'Your AOL Account …', purporting to be from service@aol.com, which says 'to enjoy your AOL experience and keep your account active, you must enter new, *valid* credit card information …' and asks the recipient to click on http://www.aolaccount tupdate.com; and even an email apparently from regulations.gov, which claimed that 'Due to recent changes in Rules and Regulations it is required by Law for all internet users to identify themselves in compliance with Code of Federal Regulations (CFR) to create a secure and safer internet community' before demanding 'Please fill in this form.'

Some recent phishing emails have falsely claimed that the recipients' Visa credit card was being used by another person or that a recent credit-card transaction had been declined. Others include saying that a person has received a payment of a few hundred dollars and asking them to 'set up an account' in order to access the money or claiming that an order has been placed and requiring the recipient to enter his details in order to cancel it. The most disgusting example of the last type claims that the victim's credit card will be charged for child pornography unless they enter their credit card information to cancel the order.

Bar the last example, all of these emails make use of the appropriate corporate logos and imagery to give the appearance of authenticity.

Of course none of these emails come from the organisation that they claim to have come from. Once you click on the link you will be directed to a website that appears to belong to the relevant organisation. There you will be asked to enter any combination of the following items of personal information: your username and password, credit card information (number, PIN, bank, etc), bank details, personal information such as address, email, telephone number, driver's licence number, Social Security number, mother's maiden name, etc. In other words, all the information an identity thief could need to take over any aspect of your life. This information will be stored on a computer operated or controlled by the criminals. The machine will often be physically located on the other side of the world, usually in a country where prosecution of the offenders is more difficult and therefore less likely.

Andrea from Cleveland had £6,000 stolen from her account after following the instructions in one such email. She told the BBC Radio 4's *Money Box* programme: 'You just feel so stupid. You feel that you have been taken in by a con that should have been glaringly obvious.'

There are three key components to a successful phishing email. They are:

1 Disguising the source of the email.
2 Disguising the destination website pointed to in the link
3 Creating a plausible appearing website to harvest your details.
4 Getting the emails to the potential victims.

Disguising the source of the email

This is actually much easier than it appears. All emails consist of two parts. The part that we see when we read an email is called the body. This is whatever is typed in as the text of the email, together with any attached files, such as pictures, spreadsheets, etc.

Immediately preceeding this, however, is a part of the email that we don't usually look at called the headers. The headers contain information about the email, such as to whom it is addressed, the sender, the subject line, the date, and other information such as the computers it passed through on its way from the sender to the recipient. Much of this information is used by law enforcement agencies as part of the forensic analysis process when building a case.

Here we are concerned with the header showing the sender's details, the 'From' field. While much of the header information is fixed, the contents of the From field can be set in the email program. This is called 'spoofing the From address'. The details of the technique are different for each email program, but the process is very easy. Here I shall demonstrate just how easy, using Microsoft Outlook Express, as it is probably one of the most common email applications in use today.

Spoofing the 'From' address in an email

1   In Outlook Express select the 'Tools' menu item;
2   Select the 'Accounts' option;
3   Click on the 'Mail' tab;
4   Select the default email account;
5   Click the 'Properties' button;
6   Click on the 'General' tab;
7   Find the section marked 'User Information' – your name should be in a box entitled 'Name';
8   Change the text in this box to something else – 'ID Thief' for example;
9   Click 'OK' then 'Close'.

Now send yourself an email – you'll see that it appears to come from a person or organisation called 'ID Thief'.

Don't forget to repeat the above process in order to put back your name!

Many people who are knowledgeable about computer security choose to use an alternative email program in place of Outlook, citing security vulnerabilities. I personally do not use Microsoft Outlook or Outlook Express. Many other packages are available at legitimate download sites such as http://tucows.com/ or http://www.download.com/.

Disguising the destination website

The second part of the process is a little more complicated. Take a look at the phishing email printed below, one of many I've received.

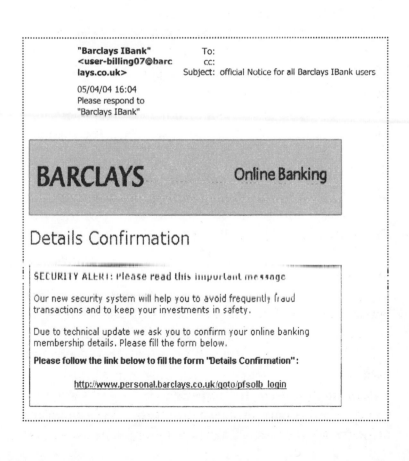

"Barclays IBank" <user-billing07@barc lays.co.uk>	To: cc: Subject: official Notice for all Barclays IBank users

05/04/04 16:04
Please respond to
"Barclays IBank"

BARCLAYS Online Banking

Details Confirmation

SECURITY ALERT: Please read this important message

Our new security system will help you to avoid frequently fraud transactions and to keep your investments in safety.

Due to technical update we ask you to confirm your online banking membership details. Please fill the form below.

Please follow the link below to fill the form "Details Confirmation":

http://www.personal.barclays.co.uk/goto/pfsolb_login

The link, http://www.personal.barclays.co.uk/goto/pfsolb_login appears to point to a genuine website, that belonging to Barclays Bank. In fact, however, analysis of the code from which the email is made up shows that the link will actually take you to an entirely different bogus website, http://www.personal.barclays.co.uk.userset.net:4903/b/index.htm. This is actually a relatively simple example to find out. Were you to position your mouse over a similar link, your email software will probably show you the real address, giving you some warning that the link is bogus.

There are, of course, more artful ways of forging links. Examples of these methods include:

IP Address

Computers on the internet, like computers everywhere, prefer to think in numbers rather than words. For example, when you type the address http://www.google.com into your web browser, it goes away and looks in a list called the Domain Name System for a number. At the time of writing, the corresponding number (called an IP or Internet Protocol address) is '216.239.59.99'. Try typing that number, with the dots, into your web browser – you should get google. Because we can't read IP addresses, scammers often use them to conceal the destination of a link in a phishing email.

The @ symbol

When the protocols that govern the way that the world wide web operates were written, the designers created a feature called automatic authentication. It allowed addresses of the form http://myname:mypassword@www.website.com.

Putting that address into a web browser would take you to the website www.website.com and then automatically enter your username and password. If login was not required then the irrelevant data would be ignored.

Now consider the following address: http://www.citibank.com @www.evilthief.com. Because of the standards described above, this link will in fact take you to www.evilthief.com *not* www.citibank.com.

Other numeric codes

There are many other ways of coding web addresses numerically so as to obscure the true address from human view. Another phishing email claimed to have come the Halifax. The link appeared to lead to: http://www.halifax-online.co.uk/_mem_bin/FormsLogin.asp?source=halifax.co.uk.

In fact it pointed to: http://%68%61%6C%69%66%61%78%2D%6F%6E%6C%69%6E%65%63%6F%75%6B%2E%7O%65%2E%6B%67. This translates as http://halifax-onlinecouk.pe.kg/ and leads to a computer in the Kyrgyz Republic in the Former Soviet Union.

Creating a plausible website

The starting point for this stage of the criminals' plan is usually a visit to the legitimate website belonging to the bank or other organisation he plans to target. There he can harvest all of the graphics and corporate branding elements he needs to make his spoof site appear genuine. Many thieves stop there, simply building their own site and moving on to the next phase of their crime. Two recent tactics, however, deserve a further mention.

The fake error message

A recent phishing scam, targeting customers of an online payments service, went one stage further. The scam started out in the usual way. Victims received an email purporting to come from their payment service and asking them to enter their details. Clicking on the link in the email took them to a website, operated by the criminal, designed to look just like the legitimate site. There the victims could give away all their personal information. Once they had done so, and clicked the button to submit, the process took a rather clever turn. Having recorded all the victim's personal information, the fake website then produced a message saying that there had been an error logging them in and asking them to click a link to try again. This new link, however, took the victim to the real payment company's genuine website. Here the victim could log into his or her real account where, finding everything in order, they would likely conclude that all was well and go about their business unaware that they had been conned, until it was far too late.

The real website

The trickiest example of a phishing site seen so far in 2004 came disguised as another message from Citibank. Clicking on the visible link http://web.da-us.citibank.com actually took victims to a fake website at http://citibank-vali date.info/. The clever part was that this site would redirect victims immediately to http://www.citibank.com, the legitimate Citibank site.

However, at the same time the fake site would also launch a pop-up window, which presented itself as a login screen. The pop-up itself looked convincing and was entirely consistent with the policy described in the message. Using this approach, the phisher eliminated one of the strongest clues of phishing – the faked address.

Getting the emails to the potential victims

Here the criminals borrow a technique from another group of unsavoury people – 'spammers'. In the context of the internet, 'spam' is defined as unsolicited bulk email. Anyone with an email account can hardly have failed to become familiar with the electronic equivalent of junk email over recent years. Because the cost of sending the emails is so close to zero it makes no difference, spammers can send millions of junk messages, only needing a few replies to make the exercise profitable. Similarly, phishers only need a small percentage of the recipients of their email to follow the instructions in order to steal significant amounts of money.

How to protect yourself

If you get an email that warns you, with little or no notice, that an account of yours will be shut down unless you recon-firm your billing information, do not reply or click on the link in the email. Treat any other email of the types described above in the same manner. Instead, contact the company cited in the email using a telephone number or website address you know to be genuine.

Avoid emailing personal and financial information. Before submitting financial information through a website, look for the 'lock' icon on the browser's status bar. It signals that your information is secure during transmission.

Review credit card and bank account statements as soon as you receive them to determine whether there are any unauthorised charges. If your statement is late by more than a couple of days, call your credit card company or bank to confirm your billing address and account balances.

The United States Department of Justice gives the following advice:

The Department of Justice recommends that internet users follow three simple rules when they see emails or websites that may be part of a phishing scheme: Stop, Look, and Call.

1. Stop. Phishers typically include upsetting or exciting (but false) statements in their emails with one purpose in mind. They want people to react immediately to that false information, by clicking on the link and inputting the requested data before they take time to think through what they are doing. Internet users, however, need to resist that impulse to click immediately. No matter how upsetting or exciting the statements in the email may be, there is always enough time to check out the information more closely.

2. Look. Internet users should look more closely at the claims made in the email, think about whether those claims make sense, and be highly suspicious if the email asks for numerous items of their personal information such as account numbers, usernames or passwords. For example:

🔒　　If the email indicates that it comes from a bank or other financial institution where you have a bank or credit-card account, but tells you that you have to enter your account information again, that makes no sense. Legitimate banks and financial institutions already have their customers' account numbers in their records. Even if the email says a customer's account is being terminated, the real bank or financial institution will still have that customer's account number and identifying information.

🔒 If the email says that you have won a prize or are entitled to receive some special 'deal', but asks for financial or personal data, there is good reason to be highly suspicious. Legitimate companies that want to give you a real prize don't ask you for extensive amounts of personal and financial information before you're entitled to receive it.

3. Call. If the email or website purports to be from a legitimate company or financial institution, internet users should call or email that company directly and ask whether the email or website is really from that company. To be sure that they are contacting the real company or institution where they have accounts, credit-card accountholders can call the toll-free customer numbers on the backo of their cards, and bank customers can call the telephone numbers on their bank statements.

☞ A report from the Metropolitan Police Intelligence Briefing

The Winter 2003/4 SO6 intelligence briefing highlights a pornographic website based in Latvia that specialises in 'Live Adult Only Video Conferencing', which found another way to boost its profits. It sold its complete list of clients together with their credit card details and addresses. Shortly afterward the following email began to circulate, sent as usual from fake or disposable email addresses.

Important Notice
We have just charged your credit card for money laundry in amount of $234.65 (because you are either child pornography webmaster or deal with dirty money, which require us to layndry [sic] them and then send to your checking account. If you feel this transaction was made by our mistake, please press 'No'. If you confirm this transaction, please press 'yes' and fill in the form below.

What banks and companies can do
In the US both the Federal Trade Commission and the Department of Justice offer guidance to consumers on avoiding phishing scams.

In November 2003 tech firm Tumbleweed Communications and a number of member banks, financial services institutions and e-commerce providers founded the Anti-Phishing Working Group (APWG), an industry association focused on eliminating the identity theft and fraud that result from the growing problem of phishing and email spoofing. The organisation provides a forum to discuss phishing issues, define the scope of the phishing problem in terms of hard and soft costs, and share information and best practices for eliminating the problem. Where appropriate, the APWG also looks to share this information with law enforcement.

Meanwhile, law enforcement sources believe organised crime gangs from Eastern Europe are the prime movers behind phishing. In May 2004 the UK's National Hi-Tech Crime Unit (NHTCU) arrested a dozen men and women, all from countries in the Former Soviet Union, including Estonia, Latvia, Lithuania, Russia and Ukraine, on suspicion of laundering funds stolen from victims of phishing attacks. The NHTCU believes the suspects were recruited by Russian organised crime gangs to open UK bank accounts into which money stolen via phishing attacks was transferred before being moved to Russian accounts. It is alleged that the 12 collected seven per cent each of the money for their trouble.

Keystroke logging

♪ The Kinko's conman

In July 2003 JuJu Jiang, a 25-year-old resident of Queens, New York, pleaded guilty in federal court to two counts of computer fraud and one charge of unauthorised possession of access codes. Jiang admitted planting copies of a commercial keyboard-logging program Invisible KeyLogger Stealth on computers at 13 Kinko's stores (internet cafés) around Manhattan.

For almost two years ending last December, Jiang harvested over 450 online banking passwords and user names from victims whose only mistake was to access their bank accounts from the internet cafés. According to the prosecution, Jiang used his victims' financial information to open new accounts under their names, then transferred their money from their legitimate accounts into the new, fraudulent ones.

When the US Secret Service raided Jiang's apartment, they seized books on hacking, a laptop computer and four desktop machines from Jiang's bedroom. Under questioning, Jiang admitted 'sniffing' passwords and usernames from Kinko's machines and selling them over the internet. Two months later, while free on bail, Jiang got caught planting another keyboard sniffer at a Kinko's on West 40th Street in New York.

Keystroke loggers come in two varieties. They are either small hardware devices or software programs, and both do the same thing. Keystroke loggers sit invisibly in the background while you use your computer, giving you no sign whatsoever of their presence. Yet these sneaky devices record every key you press, storing up everything you type from letters to login names and passwords.

Hardware keystroke loggers

These are tiny devices that sit between the keyboard and the computer. They are available for as little as $89 and some models are indistinguishable from a standard keyboard plug. The criminal has to have physical access to the back of the computer. He unplugs the keyboard, plugs the keystroke logger into the keyboard socket and then plugs the keyboard into a duplicate socket on the keystroke logger. The device will sit there and record up to a year's worth of typing. When he's ready to retrieve the data the thief can either remove the device and take it to his own machine, or simply download the information to disk directly from the target machine, leaving the device in place to snare more unwitting victims.

Software keystroke loggers

In order to install a hardware keystroke logger the criminal has to obtain physical access to your computer. While this can be possible in a shared space, such as an office or internet café, it is vastly more difficult when it comes to your home PC. This difficulty has given rise to a new generation of software keystroke loggers, invisible programs that, once installed and activated, run in the background on your computer, covertly recording every key you hit and storing the results in a hidden file. Software keystroke loggers are often referred to as an example of a type of software called 'spyware; malicious programs that hide on your computer, gathering information that they report back to their master.

♂ Spyware student stole from friends

In 2003 Wong Ming Liang and Lim Xiao Jing, two students at the National University of Singapore, received an email message from fellow student Nguyen Van Phi Hung. The email invited them to play an online game and included an attached file, 'bubble.exe'.

Unbeknown to the two victims, Hung had surreptitiously attached a hidden keystroke logger, called Perfect Keylogger, to the program. By examining the results from his hidden spyware, Hung was able to obtain access details for Mr Liang's online bank account, as well as the login-ID and password for Mr Jing's university computer account.

In late 2003 Hung used Mr Lim's university computer account to access Mr Wong's bank account. With the details he had stolen, including Mr Wong's PIN, he was able to siphon money from the account, buying pre-paid international phone cards.

In 2004, after his arrest, Hung pleaded guilty to four of eleven counts of computer misuse, admitting to having stolen US$888 from Mr Wong's bank account.

There are two stages to a keystroke logger attack: installing the logger and retrieving the data.

Installing the logger

While the methods of installing a hardware keystroke logger are very straightforward, software keystroke loggers are another matter entirely. I have said that software keystroke loggers can be described as an example of spyware. It is also fair to say that keyloggers and some spyware can be examples of a type of software known as Trojans. Named after the Greek myth about the Trojan Horse, Trojans are hidden programs that are installed on your computer by stealth, without your permission. Once present they do whatever they are programmed to, often without your knowledge.

Whatever form the keystroke logger takes, there are many methods a criminal can use to install it. Here are just a few:

Direct installation

Here the criminal simply obtains the keystroke logging program, either by buying it off the shelf or by obtaining an illegal 'pirate' copy. He then installs it on your computer in the way that one would install any piece of software. The drawback to this method is that he must gain access to your machine.

Hidden functionality

You may intentionally install a program without realising it has an unrelated, secondary purpose that isn't clearly disclosed. The most sinister examples are programs that claim to rid your computer of spyware, but in fact do exactly the opposite.

Deception

There are many malicious websites on the internet, often designed to appear high on the list of results when you search for a particular term. On accessing these websites a box will appear with a deceptive message such as 'Install this update in order to view the site'. The 'update' of course, may be nothing of the sort.

Computer virus or worm

A computer virus or worm can also install spyware that could allow a thief to log your keystrokes, steal passwords and credit card information, etc. Some viruses turn your computer into a pornography or spam server. Indeed it is believed by many that organised criminal gangs use computers hijacked in this way to distribute not only keystroke loggers but also phishing emails and other malware ('malicious software'). Such networks of suborned computers are known as 'botnets'. Organised crime gangs rent these machines out for as little as $60 for 6 hours or $2,000 per week.

Automatic installation

Some unscrupulous outfits use advertisements to automatically begin the installation process for their programs. Often the advertisements are designed to frighten you into clicking on them. They do this by looking like genuine error messages or warnings such as 'Your computer is under attack!' or 'Warning: Your internet connection is dangerously insecure. Click here to prevent infection.' Another touch is to replicate the close window button inside the advert itself, so that you can click on the advertisement without intending to.

Retrieving the information

Once the keystroke logger has been running for a while, the criminal will want to retrieve whatever it has recorded. He can do this by direct access or remote access. Direct access can be risky as he has to get physical access to the machine. For that reason many Trojans these days transfer their 'take' over the internet, either periodically when a threshold or time limit is reached or on command.

How to protect yourself

While a complete users' guide to computer security would be a book or two in itself, there are a few basic steps you can take. In this area, the only person who can do anything is you.

Make sure your system is up to date

Microsoft, Apple and other Operating System suppliers regularly make available patches and updates to ensure the security of your system and take care of newly discovered vulnerabilities. The sad fact is that a phenomenal number of users ignore them – don't! More and more Trojans, viruses, etc rely on security flaws for which patches were issued some considerable time ago.

Lock down your software

Your web browser and email client (or program) are the two most vulnerable areas here. Your browser will have security settings – check the help files. You should also turn off the automatic preview feature in your email client. Remember to carefully read pop-up warnings. If you don't expect to install a program or if you aren't sure what the program does, don't click the 'Cancel' button, but do close the window by clicking the small square x in the top right corner immediately.

Don't be promiscuous

Never download or accept files from people or websites you're not sure about. This is especially true for those downloading pirated or cracked software, so-called 'warez'. Promiscuous downloading means it's only a matter of time before you get infected.

Use protection

Installing a good anti-virus package is only part of the battle. New viruses are released all the time and anti-virus manufacturers constantly release updates to deal with them. If you don't keep your anti-virus software up to date then all it can give you is a false sense of security.

Beware of attachments in email – even from friends

Many viruses and Trojans spread by infecting emails and sending themselves to contacts in the email address book. Always check if an attachment is unexpected.

Windows – watch out for hidden file extensions
Often, especially on Windows systems, Trojans will masquerade as pictures, music or other harmless files. Make sure you know what it is before you open it.

Additional protection
Run a spyware detector and a firewall. There are many good, free or cheap versions of both available. The firewall can be particularly useful in preventing or alerting you to a Trojan's attempt to send its 'take' back to its master. To learn more about firewalls and security visit http://www.grc.com/lt/score boardhtm.

What banks and companies can do
There is a solution to the problem of keystroke loggers. It's called two-factor authentication and is already used by banks in Switzerland, Germany and many other European countries.

Customers with online access to their bank accounts are issued with a small electronic device that generates a different password each time it's used or a plastic card with a number of scratch-off panels, behind each of which is a different password. A master list of these passwords is held on the bank's computer. Each time they want to access their account they must type in their username, password and the next password from their card or device. Each of these passwords is usable only once.

Whereas a traditional username and password system confirms your identity by means of 'something you know' (your password), two-factor authentication requires 'something you know PLUS something you have'. Even if a keystroke logger captures the second password when you type it in, that is of no use to the identity thief because the bank has now flagged that password as used and wants the next one on the list – and the thief doesn't have the card.

In the UK and US use of two-factor authentication is largely limited to securing employee access to corporate networks. There have been limited consumer trials, but banks are concerned about balancing security with ease of use. Ultimately the banks are worried that whichever goes first will be perceived by customers as making life too hard and so lose business to their competitors.

Account Hijacking

♪ eBay antics

In December 2002 Kevin tried to log into his eBay account, but found he was locked out. Every time he entered his details he was told his password was incorrect. This had Kevin worried – apart from anything else, he wanted to find out why he had email from 18 eBay users, all wanting to buy camcorders from him. Camcorders he'd never advertised.

By the time eBay was able to shut down Kevin's account it was too late. The fraudsters had taken the money and run, leaving victims like Kansas City audio engineer Craig $605 out of pocket and Kevin to deal with all the negative feedback and damage to his eBay reputation.

Kevin's eBay account had been hijacked. Account hijacking could be described as the online equivalent of the account takeover techniques we saw earlier in this book. Once the thieves had access to Kevin's account, by somehow obtaining his password, they were able to masquerade as him, while changing the password to lock him out.

Online account hijackers typically target auction service accounts and email accounts but their activity is not limited to those accounts alone. Other prime targets are online bank accounts, other online payment services, such as PayPal, and e-commerce accounts such as those with online retailers or travel agents.

♪ Dan's Story

'In August 2002 someone using an email address from a free email service managed to hack my PayPal password and add his/her email address. This individual then removed my email addresses, blocking me from access to my business account.

'Fortunately, I usually have less than $100 in my PayPal account. Unfortunately, that PayPal account is also linked to my business checking account.

'So all it takes for someone to clear out my business account is guessing my password, adding their email address, and then removing my access to the account before I have a chance to respond. And that's exactly what happened.

'Do I recommend against using PayPal? No, or at least not yet. The service is very convenient. Users need to be much more aware of the pitfalls. Make sure your password is obscure, and don't keep much money in the bank account linked to your PayPal account.'

To take over an online account the criminals need, at minimum, a login-ID and a password. Clearly the two methods described above can provide both, but there are a number of other ways by which they can gain access.

Publicly available login-IDs

Often our login-ID is public knowledge. For eBay accounts, the login-ID is the same as our seller-ID. For Yahoo!Mail it is the part of the email address immediately preceding the '@'. For many other systems, including sensitive accounts such as PayPal, the publicly available email address is used. Many airline sites use our frequent flyer number which, while less readily available, often conforms to a known standard and is often displayed on luggage tags.

Weak passwords

Having found or deduced our login ID, the criminals' next challenge is to obtain our password. Many people use ordinary words or dates as their passwords. Identity thieves are aware of this, of course, and use automated programs to try one word after another until they meet with success. Because these attacks often use dictionary files from spell checker routines they are known as dictionary attacks.

Duplicate passwords

Many people use the same password for multiple accounts. Once a criminal has found the password to one of your accounts he will try it with as many other accounts as he can.

Forgotten password vulnerabilities

Most systems offer a facility to assist users who have forgotten their password. This can be exploited in a number of ways. Some sites will email the password to the registered email address when asked. If the thief has already gained access to your email account he simply need ask for a password reminder and wait for the key to be handed to him. Other sites allow the user to present alternative credentials in lieu of their password. The information asked for might be credit card details, pet's name, mother's maiden name, etc. If the thief has any of this information (and much of it is publicly available; how many of us regard our pet's name as a secret?) then he is in a position to hijack your account.

Sophisticated technological attacks

There is no such thing as a 100 per cent secure system. Technologically aware criminals will, from time to time, bypass the security of a system and steal user data. This process is often mis-referred to as 'hacking'.

How to protect yourself

Some things are beyond our control, such as where an online service has a rigorous login-ID policy. But there are a few things you can do.

Choose strong passwords

That is, choose passwords that contain letters, numbers and symbols (!,#%&, etc). Don't use words found in the dictionary or any combination that is easy to guess, such as 'qwerty' or '1234'. Passwords should be at least 8 characters long and be composed of as many different types of character (upper and lower case letters, numbers, other symbols if allowed) as you can remember. There are a number of techniques for coming up with memorable, strong passwords. I'll give an example; you can go through as many of these stages as you want.

1. First make up a 'nonsense' word, one that is easy for you to remember, but difficult for others to guess. One way of doing this is with mnemonics, taking the first letter of each word of a memorable phrase. This could be a line from a poem or a song, or something more personal. For example:

-   'The Listeners' by Walter De La Mare begins: '"Is there anybody there?" said the Traveller, Knocking on the moonlit door.' Taking the first letter of each word gives us 'itatsttkotmd'.

-   While the last stanza of Robert Frost's 'Stopping by Woods on a Snowy Evening' begins 'The woods are lovely, dark and deep, But I have promises to keep', which gives us 'twaldadbihptk'.

-   Either of these would make decent passwords, but we can make them stronger and still memorable. For the next stage let's pretend our word was 'bimblebrod'.

2. Take your word and use it, in combination with different numbers for your passwords. Have you noticed that some numbers look like letters?

Replacing 'i' with '1' and 'o' with '0' gives us 'b1mblebr0d'.

3. Now insert a memorable, but non-obvious number; say you were born in 1965. You don't want to use '1965' or '65'; someone who knows when you were born will try those. So just take your '65' and do something systematic with it. For example '65' is a '5' after a '6' or a '6' before a '5':

   either put a '5' after the sixth character, giving 'b1mble 5br0d'.

   or put a '6' before the fifth character, to give 'b1mb 6lebr0d'.

4. Finally come up with a substitution you can remember, say 'always replace "L" with "*"'. That gives us 'b1mb*e5br0d' or 'b1mb6*ebr0d' While these passwords look complex and unguessable, they are actually quite memorable if you remember the stages to go through.

Use different passwords for different accounts
Once the crooks have one of your passwords that works they will try this against every other account you have, in the hope that you've used it more than once.

Choose strong login-IDs
Wherever possible choose a login-ID that is less than obvious – avoid email addresses. Your email address is one of the first login-IDs a thief will try, along with your name.

Don't use the 'remember this password' feature on your computer

Anybody gaining access to your machine, while you're out for example, could log in to your accounts and change the passwords, letting him plunder them at his leisure.

Change your passwords regularly

Many security experts recommend once every two to four months.

Use a credit card rather than a debit card wherever possible

Credit card provide marginally better protection if compromised.

Use obscure reminder questions and answers

Don't have 'What's my favourite team?' if there's a picture of them on your desktop and don't use your mother's maiden name. Be devious. If you have to use 'What's my city of birth?' pick a small town nearby and remember the deception.

Advance fee fraud

The email overleaf is typical of several I receive each week:

"PRINCE JIM UDU WEST" <jim222@asurfer.com>   To: cc: Subject: ASSISTANCE.

13/05/04 03:11
Please respond to
princejimudu

VERY URGENT INVESTMENT TRANSACTION.

DEAR PARTNER,

IN ORDER TO TRANSFER OUT (TWENTY SIX MILLIONU.S.DOLLARS)
 FROM OUR BANK. I HAVE THE COURAGE TO LOOK
FOR A RELIABLE AND HONEST PERSON WHO WILL BE CAPABLE
FOR THIS IMPORTANT TRANSACTION. BELIEVING THAT YOU
WILL NEVER LET ME DOWN EITHER NOW OR IN FUTURE.

I AM PRINCE JIM UDU WEST.THE AUDITOR AND COMPUTING
MANAGER UNITED BANK OF AFRICA [U.B.].
THERE IS AN ACCOUNT OPENED IN THIS BANK IN 1980 AND
SINCE 1990 NOBODY HAS OPERATED ON THIS ACCOUNT AGAIN,
AFTER GOING THROUGH SOME OLD FILES IN THE RECORDS,
I DISCOVERED THAT IF I DO NOT REMITT THIS MONEY OUT
URGENTELY,IT WILL BE FORFEITED FOR NOTHING.

HOW THE MONEY CAME ABOUT:

THE OWNER OF THIS ACCOUNT IS MR GAVIN LADHAMS A
FOREIGNER AND THE MANAGER OF PETROL CHEMICAL SERVICE,
A CHEMICAL ENGINEER BY PROFFESSION AND HE DIED SINCE
1980.AND THEN,SINCE 1990, NOBODY KNOWS ABOUT THIS
ACCOUNT OR ANYTHING CONCERNING IT, THE ACCOUNT HAS NO
OTHER BENEFICIARY AND MY INVESTIGATION PROVED TO ME AS
WELL THAT HIS COMPANY DOES NOT KNOW ANYTHING ABOUT
THIS ACCOUNT AND THE AMOUNT INVOLVED IS (U.S.$26,000,000.

I WANT TO TRANSFER THIS MONEY INTO A SAFE FOREIGN
ACCOUNT ABROAD BUT I DON'T KNOW ANY FOREIGNER, I AM
ONLY CONTACTING YOU AS A FOREIGNER BECAUSE THIS MONEY
CAN NOT BE APPROVED TO ANY LOCAL BANK HERE BUT CAN
ONLY BE APPROVED TO ANY FOREIGN ACCOUNT BECAUSE THE
MONEY IS U.S DOLLARS AND THE FORMER OWNER OF THE
ACCOUNT IS MR GAVIN LADHAMS AND HE WAS A FOREIGNER TOO.

I KNOW THAT THIS MESSAGE WILL COME TO YOU AS A
SURPRISE AS WE DON'T KNOW OUR SELF BEFORE, BUT BE SURE
THAT IT IS REAL AND A GENUINE BUSINESS.I BELIEVE IN

GOD THAT YOU WILL NEVER LET ME DOWN IN THIS
INVESTMENT, YOU ARE THE ONLY PERSON THAT I HAVE
CONTACTED FOR THIS INVESTMENT FOR NOW. SO PLEASE REPLY
URGENTLY.

WHEN THE TRANSFER IS APPROVED AND PAYMENT SCHEDULE IS
ALOCATED OVERSEAS,THROUGH THE OFFSHORE PAYING
DELEGATE FOR FINAL CLEARANCE AND SIGNING OF THE
PAYMENT REALEASE FORM BY THE BENEFICIARY, I WANT US TO
SEE AT THE OVERSEA PAYING CLEARANCE OFFICE FACE TO
FACE OR SIGNING OF THE ORIGINAL BINDDING AGREEMENT TO
BIND US TOGETHER SO THAT,WE CAN RECEIVE THIS MONEY
INTO A FOREIGN ACCOUNT OR ANY ACCOUNT OF YOUR CHOICE
WHERE THE FUND WILL BE REMITTED.

I AM CONTACTING YOU BECAUSE OF THE NEED TO INVOLVE A
FOREIGNER WITH A FOREIGN ACCOUNT AS THE REAL
BENEFICIARY. I NEED YOUR CO-OPERATION TO MAKE THIS
WORK FINE, BECAUSE THE MANAGEMENT IS READY TO APPROVE
THIS PAYMENT TO ANY FOREIGNER WHO HAS THE CORRECT
INFORMATION TO THIS ACCOUNT,WHICH I WILL GIVE TO YOU
WHEN SURE OF YOUR CAPABILITY TO HANDLE SUCH AMOUNT IN
STRICT CONFIDENCE AND TRUST.

ACCORDING TO MY INSTRUCTIONS AND MY ADVICE FOR OUR
MUTUAL BENEFIT BECAUSE I DON'T WANT TO MAKE ANY
MISTAKE, I NEED YOUR STRONG ASSURANCE AND TRUST. I
SHALL DESTROY ALL DOCUMENTS CONCERNING THIS
TRANSACTIONS IMMEDIATELY WE RECEIVED THIS MONEY
LEAVING NO TRACE TO ANY PLACE.

I WILL USE MY POSITION AND INFLUENCE ON OTHER STAFFS
TO EFFECT THE LEGAL APPROVALS AND ONWARD TRANSFER OF
THIS MONEY TO YOUR ACCOUNT WITH APPROPRIATE CLEARANCE
FROM FOREIGN PAYMENT DEPARTMENT. WITH ASSURANCE THAT
THIS MONEY WILL BE INTACT PENDING MY PHYSICAL ARRIVAL
TO YOUR COUNTRY FOR THE SHARING AND OTHER INVESTMENT.
AT THE CONCLUSION OF THIS INVESTMENT, YOU WILL BE
GIVEN 25% OF THE TOTAL AMOUNT,WHILE 70% WILL BE FOR
ME,AND 5% WILL BE FOR EXPENSES , BOTH PARTIES MIGHT
HAVE INCURED DURING THE PROCESS OF THIS TRANSACTION.
YOU CAN AS WELL MAIL ME VIA MY EMAIL ALTERNATIVE
{jimudu@asurfer.com} I AM WAITING FOR YOU URGENT
RESPONS.

THANK

PRINCE JIM UDU.

If it is to be believed I stand to make 25 per cent of $26 million ($8.5 million) simply for allowing somebody to funnel money through my bank account. If this sounds too good to be true, then that's because it is – far too good to be true.

Although this is only peripherally an identity theft crime I feel it worth including, both for completeness and because it is a scam that has claimed lives. 'Advance fee fraud', also known as '419 fraud' after the section of the Nigerian Criminal Code that makes it illegal, is an old crime in new clothes. The US Secret Service estimates that the crime is worth hundreds of millions of dollars each year. Scotland Yard reports that some victims, having lost so much themselves, become 'part of the gang', recruiting more victims from their own country of residence. According to the Metropolitan Police Fraud Squad, there are tragic cases of victims being unable to cope with the losses and committing suicide.

Originally known as the 'Nigerian letter scam', advance fee fraud has migrated to the internet with a vengeance. The criminals have used a great many scenarios to hook their victims but some aspects are common to most of the scams.

The initial contact

The email will arrive out of the blue. The sender will often apologise for contacting you out of the blue, saying that he was given your address by a mutual business acquaintance, or found you through an international business directory and knows you to be an honest man of good character. Note that the 'honest man of good character' reference is often used even where the potential victim is a woman.

The criminal's references

Of course it would not do for the letter to come from a mere nobody. The sender typically identifies himself as a Prince, Chief, General, Professor, government minister, senior official of a bank or large corporation or the relative of a recently deceased dictator. After the second Gulf War a number of these letters purported to come from one of Saddam Hussein's daughters.

The money

The sender is aware of a substantial amount of money, which nobody else knows about. Sometimes the money is in an account opened by a 'foreigner', now deceased. Other times it is a government or corporate slush fund or money hidden away by a former dictator or military strong man. It is always a large amount, rarely less than $25 million and usually more than $35 million.

Your help

The sender then explains that he cannot retrieve the money himself. This may be, as in the example above, because the money 'can only be paid to a foreigner'. Alternatively, he may be forbidden from opening a foreign bank account himself, due to his position as a government official, or unable to come out of hiding for fear of being killed. The excuses are endless, but in each case he needs to move the money through your bank account in order to access it.

Your cut

In exchange for your help, you are to receive a share of the money, typically one quarter to one third. This is, of course, millions of dollars. The money will be paid once 'matters are satisfactorily concluded'. Unbelievably, this bait is sufficiently tempting to draw in a number of victims.

Secrecy and urgency

The final common factors are twofold. First you are enjoined to keep this completely confidential. If anyone else were to find out the money would be taken by others and your opportunity would be lost. Second, there is always a need for urgency. If you do not act quickly, the money will be forfeited, discovered by others, etc.

The scam is run in up to three distinct stages. First the scammers hook their victim. Next, unexpected problems arise, requiring the victim to supply funds. Finally the victim is asked to travel to a meeting to finalise the deal.

Hooking the victim

When somebody is foolish enough to reply to one of these 419 letters a machine swings into action. The victim is asked to demonstrate his identity and bonafides. After all, the sender of the letter is about to trust him with a great deal of money. So, the victim is required to provide bank details, letterheads, etc. In return for these useful items (which the scammers will use to forge letters of recommendation to other victims or apply for travel visas) the victim is supplied with forged documents demonstrating the existence and availability of the money. The goal is to string out the process, while giving the victim an increasing sense of involvement and personal investment in the scheme. According to Scotland Yard: 'Those who contact the fraudsters are about to participate in a "hurdle" race with each hurdle increasing in size as the victim is thwarted each time he is close to the end. By the time the victim has overcome all the hurdles he is in such a state of involvement that he is practically throwing his money at the fraudsters just to finish the course.'

Unexpected problems – the advance fee

When the criminals are sure their victim is hooked it is time to move to the next stage. The US Secret Service has this to say: 'Some alleged problem concerning the "inside man" will suddenly arise. An official will demand an up-front bribe or an unforeseen tax or fee to the Nigerian government will have to be paid before the money can be transferred. These can include licensing fees, registration fees, and various forms of taxes and attorney fees. Normally each fee paid is described as the very last fee required. Invariably, oversights and errors in the deal are discovered by the Nigerians, necessitating additional payments and allowing the scheme to be stretched out over many months.'

The visit

Many 419 frauds stop at the second stage. Those that continue to the third stage are far more sinister. When the fraudsters believe they are approaching the point of diminishing returns it is time for the 'coup de grace'. The victim is invited to travel to a meeting to receive the money. This is often in Nigeria or a border country, although in recent years London, South Africa, Spain and Amsterdam have become popular. Even in the least sinister cases this tactic provides the criminals with several advantages. Firstly they can control the area where the meeting will be held. Control of the area, plus the victim's unfamiliarity with it gives them a measure of control over the victim. Secondly, if something should go wrong, they can rely on jurisdictional problems within the law to help frustrate any prosecution. Victims attending such meetings have had further money extorted in return for worthless forged cheques, been robbed, kidnapped and held for ransom or even murdered.

♪ Fraudsters caught – a global crime

The criminals operating 419 scams are happy to work globally as the two cases below, reported on the Metropolitan Police's FraudAlert website show. The first features two criminals operating in the UK but robbing victims around the world. In the second, the criminals were in South Africa, while the victims were in the UK.

> Kevin Shaun Granshaw, a 34-year-old builder, and Anthony Abedamibo, 31 years old and unemployed, appeared before His Honour Judge Jackson at Southwark Crown Court, where they initially pleaded not guilty to three counts of Conspiracy to Defraud and two counts of Assault with Intent to Resist Arrest.
>
> After hearing evidence from witnesses from America, India and Switzerland over four days, the defendants changed their pleas to guilty on the first conspiracy matter. The two further counts of conspiracy were withdrawn and

the assault matters left to lie on file. Both were sentenced to 12 months' imprisonment (6 months to be served and the remainder on licence).

In October 2000 the officers were informed of an Indian victim who had paid £17,438 to the suspects on a West African Letter Fraud. The suspects were asking for a further £100,000. The defendants were arrested after a police operation.

His Honour Judge Jackson commended the SCD6 Economic and Specialist Crime OCU officers for the conduct of the enquiry, for being alert, ingenious and displaying a degree of courage. His Honour went on to say that, '... such offences were prevalent and caused loss to the victims and to the public purse,' also that 'such investigations should be encouraged ...'.

On 12.10.00, Michael Edoho and Mike Okoyee appeared before Johannesburg Regional Court charged with two offences of Fraud arising from their arrest in connection with an Advance Fee fraud against UK nationals. Both had been arrested in January 2000 following a joint operation between SCD6 Economic and Specialist Crime OCU and the South African Police Service.

Ldoho admitted the offences and following mitigation was sentenced to 8 years' imprisonment. Okoye, who at the time of his arrest was also wanted concerning drug trafficking offences, had been remanded to await sentence following his forthcoming trial on the drugs matter.

This was the first successful prosecution of such an Advance Fee fraud in South Africa and came about solely due to the UK witnesses attending court. It is thought that these criminals have been operating in South Africa due to the success of SCD6 Economic and Specialist Crime OCU in tackling this type of crime in London.

As noted above, advance fee fraudsters use a vast number of stories and personas to hook their victims. In addition there are three substantial variations on the scam.

The lottery winner

This variant begins with an email bringing you the good news that you have won several million dollars in a lottery. Often the email claims that it was a Dutch or Spanish lottery, although other countries are also used. Upon replying the victims are first asked to 'verify their identity'. This involves filling in a form giving personal information and providing copies of passport, driving licence, etc. In other words, all the criminals need to commit full scale identity theft.

In the next stage, victims are offered three options to collect their 'winnings'. These are:

1. Have the money transferred to your own bank account – in which case you are required to provide your bank details, along with an advance fee (for taxes, insurance, legal fees, etc). Of course, no money will enter your account, but some may well leave it!
2. Open an online account with a bank specified by the lottery. This 'bank', which is of course fake, will require an opening deposit of several thousand dollars. That is the last you'll see of the money.

3 Collect your winnings in person. Here you get to travel to Amsterdam, hand over a 'release fee' in cash and, if you're lucky, leave with a bundle of worthless, counterfeit currency.

A variation on the lottery scam told victims that they had won the Massachusetts State Lottery. In a clever twist, victims were given a username and password and directed to a website, www.mass-lottery.org, which imitates the real Massachusetts State Lottery site, at www.masslottery.com

On logging in, victims were told 'If you are a US resident, not a resident of the State of Massachusetts you'll be required to pay the $500.00 gaming tax. If you are receiving from outside the United States you will have to pay $100.00 foreign gaming tax.' I've corrected the spelling errors.

Of course victims were then asked to provide their credit card details, Social Security number, and other information valuable to identity thieves.

Black money

According to Scotland Yard, this is a favourite old method, often used as a continuance of or in conjunction with advance fee fraud. The victim is shown a suitcase full of black, banknote-sized pieces of paper. He is told that this is genuine money (normally $100 bills), coated with a special substance in order to smuggle them out of the country. The victim is invited to purchase 'a very special cleaning solution' at a cost between $20,000 and $500,000 to return the notes to their original status (the criminals seem to prefer working in US dollars).

♪ A typical case

The Job, the official magazine of the London Metropolitan Police Service, reported the case of 34-year-old Tony Adej, who pleaded guilty at Wood Green Crown Court in July 2003 to going equipped to steal.

Adej was arrested on January 30 at a rented storage facility in Ruislip, Middlesex while engaged in a typical 'black money' scam. Police seized two metal trunks containing 'black money'. The victim, who was present at the time of arrest, was a man who claimed to have handed over a total of £100,000 in advance fees.

Adej had taken previous victims to the same storage facility and shown them the same two metal trucks containing the 'black money'. These previous incidents had been captured on the storage company's CCTV and witnessed by employees at the storage facility, who also identified Adej as the person concerned and the person who had rented the facility under a false name.

During interview Adej claimed that he had only been in the United Kingdom for three days prior to his arrest. However, the CCTV evidence captured him visiting the facility on three separate occasions over a six-week period prior to his arrest.

He was sentenced to 12 months' imprisonment.

The scam works like this. The fraudster will 'randomly select' three or four of the notes, then clean them with a sample of the special solution. They will be revealed as genuine $100 bills, which the victim is invited to take to a bank, in order to have their authenticity confirmed. In fact, these are the only genuine notes in the entire suitcase and their selection was anything but random. The rest are just pieces of black paper. The blackening effect is caused by a solution of petroleum jelly in iodine and the 'special cleaning fluid' is just washing-up liquid (dish soap), mixed with any other fluid of unusual colour or smell.

Cashier's cheque excess

This variant on advance fee fraud is particularly clever because it appears to run in reverse. As far as the victim is aware, it is he who has received the advance fee and therefore has nothing to worry about. Because of United States banking regulations it is particularly popular there.

The fraudsters will identify somebody selling a high-value item, such as a car or motor cycle, often via an online auction site. After agreeing to your price they will offer to pay by cashier's cheque (banker's draft). When you accept their offer the sting begins. The 'buyer' will tell you that he has a cashier's cheque for $10,000 to $15,000 more than the agreed amount, because it is a repayment of a debt or an insurance payout, or for some other reason. He will offer to give you this cheque, and trust you to wire him the difference (usually via Western Union or some other money transfer service) once the cheque has cleared.

The thieves rely on a time lag between the deposited 'funds' becoming available to you (two working days in the USA) and the cheque actually clearing (two weeks). The cashier's cheque is, of course, a forgery. After you've wired the money, you'll find the whole value deducted from your balance when the forgery becomes apparent.

How to protect yourself

While many of the crimes described in this book have a certain subtlety that explains how the victims are taken in, this type of online crime, particularly the '419' scam, is an exception. Really, how likely is it that somebody, of whom you've never heard before, is going to contact you out of the blue and offer you a few million dollars for nothing? It's not remotely likely, is it? As for the lottery scam, the thing about winning lotteries is that you have to enter them first. You give them money and get a ticket. No money, no ticket. No ticket, no prize. And you didn't buy a ticket, did you?

This type of crime depends upon a suspension of disbelief on the part of the victim. But it's a phenomenal leap. So don't make it.

The simplest way to avoid this con is don't reply to the emails. Just delete them. If you wish, and have the technical skill, forward them to the appropriate abuse address at the relevant ISP. But be careful – the example quoted at the beginning of this section mentions two email addresses, one in the text of the email and one in the headers. Further examination of the headers reveals yet a third ISP being used. Always include the full headers when forwarding fraud emails.

Remember, legitimate operations don't send you spam emails asking for sensitive personal information. At least they shouldn't, and if one does, you might consider asking yourself how seriously they take information security.

The police

The Metropolitan Police Fraud Squad at New Scotland Yard has a specialist 419 unit. Their website is http://

www.met.police.uk/fraudalert/419.htm. However, they don't want copies of every advance fee fraud email ever sent. Their website asks 'Unless your letter/email contains details of the fraudsters bank accounts/addresses/telephone numbers please do not forward them to us.'

The US Secret Service has information available at http://www.secretservice.gov/alert419.shtml.

Chapter 10

What to do if you've become a Victim of Identity Theft

As the preceding chapters show, we are all at risk of becoming a victim of identity theft. Although there is a great deal we can do to minimise that risk, we can never eliminate it altogether. Even if you follow all the precautions outlined in this book you could still become a victim.

So what should you do then?

How do you know if you're a victim?

Most identity theft crime is eventually discovered. But while the amount of damage the criminals can do is limited, to an extent, by the time between beginning their spree and discovery there is another equally important time window. That is the time between your personal information being stolen and it first being put to use. By minimising these two intervals we can limit or eliminate the damage.

🔒   Check your statements as soon as you receive them.

   🔒   Know when your bills and statements are due.

   🔒   Keep records, including copies of your card details and especially the telephone numbers. Some security experts recommend emptying out your wallet or purse, placing everything onto a photocopier and making a copy. Then turn it all over and repeat. Put these in a safe place.

The first step in dealing with identity theft is recognising the signs that indicate you may be a victim. I use the term 'may' because not all of the signs below are proof positive that you are, in fact, a victim of identity theft. For example, if your wallet or purse is stolen you are certainly at risk of identity theft but it does not necessarily follow that it will happen. While the thief might use your cards and identity he might be just as likely to take the cash and discard the rest. Either way, the steps you should take are the same.

The warning signs

There are three types of warning sign: things going missing, problems with your mail and unexpected things turning up.

Things going missing

   🔒   Your wallet, purse or handbag is stolen;

   🔒   Your home is burgled;

   🔒   Important documents, such as your driving licence, passport, credit card or bank statements or utility bills go missing;

   🔒   Cheques go missing from your chequebook.

Problems with your mail

- Your bank or credit card statements don't arrive when you expect them;
- Other mail, such as utility bills, doesn't arrive;
- You stop receiving mail altogether;
- Royal Mail or USPS contact you regarding a mail redirection request that you didn't make.

Unexpected things turning up

- Your bank or credit card statement shows charges or withdrawals that you didn't authorise;
- You start receiving bills or statements for purchases you didn't make or from businesses you don't shop at;
- You receive credit cards or credit card statements for cards you didn't apply for;
- You receive letters or calls saying that you've been approved or declined for credit that you didn't apply for;
- One of your creditors tells you that they've received an application for credit in your name, which you didn't make;
- You are contacted by debt collection agencies for debts that you didn't incur;
- You apply for a loan, mortgage or credit card and are turned down for reasons that don't reflect your true financial position;
- Your credit report shows information about accounts you did not open, searches by companies you did not apply to or information about addresses you have no connection to;
- Your bank or credit card company contacts you about suspicious transactions on your account;

🔒 You become aware of criminal or civil action against you for things that are nothing to do with you.

What to do

The first and most important thing is not to panic. The FTC estimates that, on average, it takes most identity theft victims 12 months to become aware of it. If the crime has been going on that long then you're unlikely to make things too much worse by taking a moment to catch your breath before acting. In the UK, authorities estimate that it takes 300 hours on average to repair the damage done by identity theft. Again a few minutes of thinking time won't hurt.

Now that you're ready to begin dealing with the problem it's important to be organised. While the details of the process vary slightly between the UK and the US the overall structure is the same. It looks like this:

🔒 Keep records;
🔒 Establish the facts;
🔒 Contact financial institutions;
🔒 Contact credit reporting/reference agencies;
🔒 Report the crime to the police and any other appropriate government or law enforcement agency;
🔒 If any of your government-issued ID has been lost or stolen report it to the appropriate issuing authority and request new documentation;
🔒 Restore your credit rating if it has been damaged;
🔒 If associated with the thief's criminal record, work with police to clear your name.

The steps above and detailed below are not intended as legal advice. While there is a great deal that you can do yourself, self-help is not a substitute for qualified legal representation. The thing about lawyers is, when you need them you really need them.

Keeping records

Identity theft cases can sometimes take a very long time to satisfactorily resolve. Worse, old problems that you thought were dealt with can reappear on your credit file years later. Because of this it's vital that you keep record of all the facts and copies of all correspondence from the beginning. The following steps will help you to organise your files:

1. Make notes of telephone conversations. Write down the date, the organisation you spoke to, the name of the person and whatever he or she told you.

2. Where appropriate follow up any telephone conversation in writing. Base the letter on your notes of the conversation, using the following structure to confirm that 'on such and such a date I spoke with so-and-so. I explained the following facts. So-and-so advised me to do such-and-such and promised to do whatever.' Send your letters registered post in the UK or certified mail in the USA. Request a receipt or other acknowledgement.

3. Keep copies of all letters or forms that you send, along with details of date posted.

4. Keep the originals of any documentation where possible. Send copies of things like police reports, etc.

5. Organise your paperwork in a filing system. This doesn't have to be complex and you should use

whatever system you feel most comfortable with. Some people like to file things by company or organisation, others prefer to organise their records by date.

6 Keep your files even when you thing everything is over. As I said above, errors can reappear on your credit report and all organisations occasionally make mistakes. If this happens to you you'll be glad you kept your files.

7 If you live in the US you should also keep a log of all costs incurred, time spent on the case and so forth. You may be able to use this in a claim for damages against the thief.

Establishing the facts

It's important not to over-react. While a visit from a debt collector for an account you didn't open is pretty solid evidence of identity theft, some of the signs are subtler. For example, if your regular credit card bills or statements don't arrive when you expect them there could be an innocent explanation. Perhaps there's a postal workers strike or perhaps your bank is late sending them out. Also, letters do occasionally go missing or get delivered to the wrong address.

Contact your bank and your mail carrier (usually the Royal Mail in the UK or the US Postal Service in the US). It may be possible to put your mind at rest with just a couple of telephone calls. In many cases, however, establishing all the facts will be an ongoing process, with more information becoming apparent at different stages.

Contacting financial institutions

The next step is to contact any and all financial institutions involved in your case. What you say to them will, of course, depend on what's happened. In all cases follow up the phone call with a letter and keep records of the time and date.

🔒 If you've had credit cards, cheques, etc stolen – call the issuing banks and ask for the cards or cheques to be cancelled. Ask the financial institution for a recent transaction history and inform them of any transactions you didn't make.

🔒 If you've noticed items on your bill that refer to transactions you didn't make – call the bank or credit company immediately to report unauthorised activity. Ask for the card to be cancelled or the account to be frozen. Again ask for a list of recent transactions not on your last statement.

🔒 If you receive bills or statements for goods, services or credit that you know you didn't ask for – contact the issuing organisation to alert them to the fraud.

🔒 If you're called by someone claiming to be from your credit card issuer or other financial institution regarding suspect transactions on your account – ask them for their name and the name of their department. Then call the organisation on a number you have for them that's either printed on your card or on a statement and ask to be put through to the appropriate person. Once you're sure that you are really speaking to your bank work with them to identify suspect transactions.

In the UK

Most banks and other financial institutions will have their own forms and paperwork for dealing with identity theft cases. Ask them to send you the necessary forms and complete and return them promptly. Keep copies for your files. Make sure the forms list all the suspect activity you're aware of and inform the organisation if any new information comes to light.

If the organisation does not have its own form you should write to them disputing the fraudulent activity and giving the following information:

- Your full name, address and date of birth if appropriate;
- A brief description of the way(s) in which you believe your identity was fraudulently used;
- The name(s), type(s) and account number(s) of any legitimate accounts you have with the organisation;
- Details of any fraudulent transactions made on your legitimate account(s) including date, merchant and amount;
- The name(s), type(s), account number(s) and date of opening of any fraudulent accounts in your name with the organisation, including the value of credit, goods or services provided on each account;
- A statement that you did not authorise anyone to use your name or personal information to seek money, credit, loans, goods or services;
- A statement that you did not receive any benefit (including money, goods or services) as a result of the events described in this declaration;
- Details about the type of personally identifying information or documentation that was stolen and when it happened;

- Whether or not you have reported the incident to the police, including the crime number allocated if you have;
- Authorisation for the organisation to release this information to the police or other law enforcement agencies to assist them in the investigation and prosecution of the person(s) responsible;
- Copies of any relevant bills, statements, police report(s) and any personal identification required by the organisation;
- A statement that the information contained in this declaration is true and complete to the best of your knowledge and belief.

If writing to a bank or other lender you can ask them to register a CIFAS entry relating to the fraud.

In the US

If the thief has misused one of your existing accounts then the process is largely the same as that in the UK. If the organisation does not have its own forms you can write giving information similar to that required in the UK. The Federal Trade Commission gives the following advice in order to take advantage of your protections under the Fair Credit Billing Act, which limits your liability for unauthorised credit card charges to $50 per card:

- Write to the creditor at the address given for 'billing inquiries', not the address for sending your payments. Include your name, address, account number and a description of the billing error, including the amount and date of the error.

🔒 Send your letter so that it reaches the creditor within 60 days after the first bill containing the error was mailed to you. Note that this is not the date you received the bill. Even if the thief changed the address on your account the clock still starts ticking on the day the creditor mailed the bill.

🔒 Send your letter by certified mail, and request a return receipt. This will be your proof of the date the creditor received the letter. Include copies (NOT originals) of sales slips or other documents that support your position. Keep a copy of your dispute letter.

🔒 The creditor must acknowledge your complaint in writing within 30 days after receiving it, unless the problem has been resolved. The creditor must resolve the dispute within two billing cycles (but not more than 90 days) after receiving your letter.

🔒 A sample letter is available at http://www.consumer.gov/idtheft/images/letter1.gif.

🔒 If the thief has opened new accounts you may be able to use the FTC's Identity Theft Affidavit. When you contact the organisation to report the fraud ask if they accept this or have their own forms. You can download a copy of the form, along with instructions for completing it from http://www.ftc.gov/bcp/conline/pubs/credit/affidavit.pdf or order a copy of *ID Theft: When Bad Things Happen to Your Good Name* from:

Consumer Response Center
Federal Trade Commission
600 Pennsylvania, NW, H-130
Washington, DC 20580
Tel: 1-877-FTC-HELP (1-877-382-4357)

Contacting credit reporting/ reference agencies

The next step is to contact your country's credit reference and reporting agencies (CRAs). There are three each in the UK and the US and you need to contact them for two reasons:

1 To obtain copies of your credit files in order to identify any fraudulent activity or incorrect information. This will enable you to report any further fraudulent activity and close the fraudulent accounts. You will also want any such information removed from your files so as to prevent damage to your credit rating.

2 To place a fraud warning or security alert on your files to help prevent further fraud.

In the UK

The first step is to request a copy of your credit file/report from the three credit reference agencies (CRAs), Experian, Equifax and Callcredit, to check the extent of the fraudster's activity. By UK law, under Section 7 of the Data Protection Act 1988, CRAs must make credit reports available for £2, although they are allowed to offer premium services for a higher fee.

Among other data, your credit file will show all credit accounts opened in your name, plus any recent applications for credit made using your details and any checks made upon your creditworthiness.

If you find evidence of further fraud, such as accounts or applications you did not make, contact the organisation straight away and request they remove the data from your credit file. If money or goods have been obtained you should repeat the procedure for contacting lenders outlined above. In some cases you can contact the credit reference agency directly and ask it to remove the entries and deal with the lenders on your behalf.

Contact details for the CRAs in the UK are:

Experian Ltd
Consumer Help Service
PO Box 9000
Nottingham NG80 7WP
Tel: 0870 241 6212
www.experian.co.uk

Experian offers a number of ways to obtain your credit report:

- 🔒 Order online, report delivered by post within seven days – £2
- 🔒 Order by telephone, report delivered by post within 7 days – £2.50
- 🔒 By post, by filling in a form available from Experian – £2
- 🔒 CreditExpert, a premium service where for £49.99 per year Experian will provide unlimited online access to your credit report and weekly alerts of any significant changes.

Equifax plc
Credit File Advice Centre,
PO Box 1140,
Bradford BD1 5US
Tel: 08705 143700
www.equifax.co.uk

Equifax offers three ways of obtaining your credit report:

- Order online, report delivered by post within 7 days – £2
- By post, by writing to Equifax giving your full name, address and most recent former addresses (up to six years) and including a personal cheque made payable to Equifax plc – £2
- The Equifax Credit Report™ – a premium service offering instant online access to your credit report – £8.25

Callcredit plc
Consumer Services Team
PO Box 491
Leeds LS3 1WZ
Tel: 0870 060 1414
www.callcredit.plc.uk

Callcredit will send you a copy of your credit report in exchange for £2 and a completed copy of their request form.

Flagging the identity theft on your file
You may request a note be added to your credit file to state you have been the victim of identity theft – this is free of charge.

You may also wish to consider CIFAS protective registration. This costs £11.75 and will result in a CIFAS warning being placed against your address marked Category '0' (which indicates that you have been recorded on the CIFAS database at your own request for your protection). CIFAS members undertaking a search against your address, prior to granting credit, will see 'CIFAS-DO

NOT REJECT-REFER FOR VALIDATION', whatever name they search for. As a result of the entry CIFAS members will verify further the identity of applicants and in some cases request further proof of identification. This may mean you personally experience delays while your credentials are fully checked out.

To apply for CIFAS protective registration contact UK credit reference agency Equifax, giving the following information:

- Your full name;
- Your date of birth;
- Your full address with postcode;
- The names of anyone else living at your address, and their date of birth;
- Your home and work telephone numbers including the dialling codes;
- A crime reference number if applicable;
- Details about why you want a Protective Registration.

You can phone Equifax on 0870 010 2091, email protective.registrationuk@equifax.com or download the form from http://www.cifas.org.uk/protreg.htm.

In the US

Like the UK, the US has three credit reporting agencies. Unlike the UK, however, the Fair Credit Reporting Act (updated in 2003 by the Fair and Accurate Credit Transactions Act) provides consumers with additional rights. On top of federal law, many states have laws that give residents even more rights. For example residents of Georgia are entitled to two free reports per calendar year while other states cap the federal maximum fee of $9 at just $1 or $2.

At time of writing, US CRAs must give you a free copy of your report if you believe that your file contains inaccurate information due to fraud. From December 2004 all US residents will be allowed one free copy of their report annually, regardless of whether fraud is suspected. The three CRAs are working to establish a system that will allow you to access all three free reports by contacting only one agency.

In addition, all US residents are entitled to one free copy during any 12-month period if they are unemployed and intend to apply for employment in the next 60 days, are on public welfare assistance or have received notice of an adverse decision (such as denial of credit, insurance or employment) within the past 60 days.

Finally all three credit reporting agencies offer a premium service where you can order reports from all three agencies from any one of them.

Among other data, your credit file will show all credit accounts opened in your name, plus any recent applications for credit made using your details and any checks made upon your creditworthiness.

If you find evidence of further fraud, such as accounts or applications you did not make, contact the organisation straight away and request it removes the data from your credit file. If money or goods have been obtained you should repeat the procedure for contacting lenders outlined above. You should also contact the credit reporting agency directly and ask it to remove the entries – this process can happen much more quickly if you have filed a police report.

Contact details for the CRAs in the US are:

Equifax

For obtaining your credit report by mail, phone or online:

PO Box 740241
Atlanta
GA 30374-0241
Tel: 800-685-1111
www.equifax.com

Hearing impaired call: 1-800-255-0056 and ask the operator to call the Auto Disclosure Line at 1-800-685-1111 to request a copy of your report.

If none of the conditions for a free or discounted report apply Equifax will charge $9 for the report.

For $29.95 the 3-in-1 Credit Report provides a single report containing information from all three agencies.

To report fraud, call and write to:

PO Box 740241
Atlanta
GA 30374-0241
Tel: 800-525-6285

Experian

For obtaining your credit report by mail, phone or online:

PO Box 2002
Allen TX 75013
Tel: 888-EXPERIAN (397-3742)
www.experian.com

If none of the conditions for a free or discounted report apply Experian will charge $9 for the report.

For $34.95 the 3 Bureau Credit Report and PLUS Score provides a single report containing information from all three agencies, along with your Experian Credit Score.

To report fraud, call and write to:

PO Box 9530
Allen TX 75013
Tel: 888-EXPERIAN (397-3742)
TDD: 1-800-972-0322

Trans Union
For obtaining your credit report by mail, phone or online:

PO Box 1000
Chester, PA 19022
Tel: 800-888-4213
www.transunion.com

If none of the conditions for a free or discounted report apply Transunion will charge $9 for the report.

For $29.95 the 3-in-1 Credit Profile Plus Free Score provides a single report containing information from all three agencies, along with your Transunion Credit Score.

To report fraud, call and write to:

Fraud Victim Assistance Division
PO Box 6790
Fullerton, CA 92634

Tel: 800-680-7289
TDD: 1-877-553-7803

Additionally all three agencies offer premium monitoring services.

Flagging the identity theft on your file

In 2003 the agencies launched a scheme where a fraud alert submitted to any one agency will be shared with the other two. Identity theft victims can make one toll-free call to any of the nationwide credit reporting companies and be confident that it will result in all three companies taking the same steps to help protect their credit information.

Each company will follow a standardised three-step process to post a security alert on the credit file, opt the victim out of pre-approved offers of credit or insurance and mail the victim a copy of his or her credit file.

Here is what the process looks like, once the victim makes a call:

- The company receiving the initial call will notify the victim of the ID fraud initiative and will electronically notify the other two credit reporting companies of the crime.
- A fraud alert will be put on the victim's credit report at all three nationwide credit reporting companies within 24 hours.
- The victim will be opted out of all pre-approved offers of credit and insurance for two years.
- The victim's request for a copy of his or her credit report will be handled in no more than three business days. Each of the three national credit reporting

companies will work with the victim to verify the information in their respective reports and to delete any fraudulent data. If the victim files a police report, the process is even quicker. The national credit reporting agencies will voluntarily expedite services for the victim by immediately deleting fraudulent data without the usual reinvestigation procedure.

🔒 The fraud alert will be displayed by each national credit reporting agency to all lenders or other users that access the reports in the future. Once notified that the consumer has been a victim of ID fraud, the lender can then avoid opening a fraudulent account.

Note: This process only works when you first place the fraud report. You'll still have to contact the agencies individually to get further copies of your reports to monitor them.

Additional steps for stolen cheques

You also should contact these major cheque verification companies. Ask that retailers who use their databases not accept your cheques.

TeleCheck – 1-800-710-9898 or 927-0188
Certegy, Inc. – 1-800-437-5120
International Check Services – 1-800-631-9656

Call SCAN (1-800-262-7771) to find out if the identity thief has been passing bad cheques in your name.

Reporting the crime to the police and any other appropriate government or law enforcement agency

Again the position here varies as you cross the Atlantic. In the UK, at time of writing, there is no central government organisation dealing with identity theft. In the US however the Federal Trade Commission has responsibility for a multi-agency identity theft programme and has put in place a number of initiatives.

In either country it is important to report the crime to the police. As well as speeding up the process of recovering from identity theft, reporting crime gives law enforcement agencies better information to track criminal trends and focus resources appropriately.

In the UK

Unless a crime is happening right now or somebody is in immediate danger do not dial 999. The 999 service is for emergencies only.

In most cases you should report the crime to your local police station. The UK has specialist police units for certain types of crime, and the nature and scale of the crime together with the location of any offence will be the main factors in deciding which police force will investigate. This is not a decision for you to make however. Most police forces prefer that any fraud complaints are made in the first instance to the local police station. Officers there will decide whether or not to refer it to a specialist team, another force, or whether a specialist agency, such as the SFO (Serious Fraud Office, who usually only deals with crimes over £1 million), should be involved.

To contact your local police you should either phone them or go to the nearest police station that has a front office open to the public. Contact details for your local police force will be in the phone book or can be obtained from http://www.police.uk/forces/default.asp.

You should always request a crime reference number or other documentation to record the incident.

If you believe mail theft is involved you should also report it to the Royal Mail Customer Enquiry Number on 08457 740740.

In the US

Please remember that 911 is an emergency number and is not for reporting non-emergency crimes.

Usually you should file a report with your local police or sheriff's department. You may also need to report it to the police in the area where the identity theft took place. The FTC offers this advice on successfully filing a police report:

- Provide documentation. Furnish as much documentation as you can to prove your case. Debt collection letters, credit reports, your notarised ID Theft Affidavit, and other evidence of fraudulent activity can help the police file a complete report.
- Be persistent. Local authorities may tell you that they can't take a report. Stress the importance of a police report; many creditors require one to resolve your dispute. Also remind them that under their voluntary 'Police Report Initiative' credit bureaus will automatically block the fraudulent accounts and bad debts from

appearing on your credit report, but only if you can give them a copy of the police report. If you can't get the local police to take a report, try your county police. If that doesn't work, try your state police.

- If you're told that identity theft is not a crime under your state law, ask to file a Miscellaneous Incident Report instead.
- Be a motivating force. Ask your police department to search the FTC's Consumer Sentinel database for other complaints in your community. You may not be the first or only victim of this identity thief. If there is a pattern of cases, local authorities may give your case more consideration.

Other agencies

You may also be able to report identity theft crimes to your local FBI or US Secret Service office. In addition you should contact your local office of the US Postal Inspection Service if you believe the mail theft was involved as part of the fraud, the Social Security Administration if you believe your SSN is being used fraudulently and the IRS if you suspect any sort of tax violation, for example someone working and not paying tax using your name and SSN.

The Federal Trade Commission

One of the most important reports you can make is to the FTC. The FTC enters all complaints received into a secure database, which is used by law enforcement agencies around the world to aggregate cases, spot patterns and track growth in identity theft. This information can then be used to improve investigations and victim assistance.

By sharing your identity theft complaint with the FTC, you will provide important information that can help law enforcement officials track down identity thieves and stop them. The FTC also can refer victim complaints to other appropriate government agencies and companies for further action.

᠂ To file a complaint or to learn more about the FTC's Privacy Policy, visit www.consumer.gov/idtheft. If you don't have access to the internet, you can call the FTC's Identity Theft Hotline: toll-free 1-877-IDTHEFT (438-4338); TDD 202-326-2502; or write to:

Identity Theft Clearinghouse,
Federal Trade Commission
600 Pennsylvania Avenue, NW
Washington, DC 20580.

Government-issued ID

If any of your government-issued ID has been lost or stolen then, in addition to reporting it to the police, you should report it to the appropriate issuing authority and request new documentation. Below I cover the process for the three most common types of document: passports, driving licences and NI/SSN cards. For other ID, such as employment or military ID, contact the issuer for advice.

Passport
In the UK

There are two different procedures for dealing with lost or stolen passports. Which one you follow will depend on whether your passport was lost or stolen in the UK or abroad. In either case having a note of your passport number would be helpful. In both cases the loss or theft of a passport must be reported to the local police in the country in which the passport was lost or stolen. Once a UK passport is reported lost or stolen it can never be legally used again. The UK Passport Service warns that any attempt to use a cancelled passport is likely to result in the holder being detained.

If your passport is lost or stolen in the UK, you should contact the UK Passport Service to report the loss or theft by filling in form LS01. UKPS recommends that you also apply for a replacement passport at the same time, although this is not mandatory. You can contact the UKPS on 0870 521 0410 or online at: http://www.ukpa.gov.uk/_1_applications/1_lost_s tolen.asp.

If your passport is lost or stolen abroad, you should contact the local police and your nearest British Consulate, Embassy or High Commission, who will be able to advise you. The Foreign and Commonwealth Office (FCO) can provide you with details of consulates abroad and can be contacted on 0870 606 0290 and at www.fco.gov.uk.

The UKPS warn that it is only able to issue and service UK passports to British nationals who are resident in the UK at the time of application. UKPS cannot accept or deal with passport applications from people who are applying outside the UK, nor can it answer queries from British Nationals living abroad. These issues should be referred to the FCO.

In the US

As with the UK, the procedure will depend on whether your passport was lost or stolen in the United States or abroad. In either case having a note of your passport number would be helpful. Once a US passport is reported lost or stolen it will be invalidated and can no longer be used for travel. Invalidated passports cannot be re-validated.

If your passport is lost or stolen in the US, you should provide detailed answers to all questions, sign and submit Form DS-64, Statement Regarding a Lost or Stolen Passport, to:

US Department of State
Passport Services, Consular Lost/Stolen Passport Section
1111 19th Street, NW
Suite 500
Washington, DC 20036
Tel: 24 hours/day 202-955-0430

The information you provide on the DS-64, Statement Regarding a Lost or Stolen Passport, will be entered in the Consular Lost/Stolen Passport System. If you recover the passport after you have reported it lost or stolen, submit it to the address listed above. When you submit it, if requested, the Department of State will cancel it and return it to you. If not requested, it will be destroyed. To replace your lost or stolen passport fill in form DS-11, available from the Department of State or follow the instructions at http://travel.state.gov/lost_stolen.html.

If your passport is lost or stolen abroad, contact the nearest US embassy or consulate for assistance. A list is available at http://travel.state.gov/links.html. Phone numbers for US embassies and consulates are also available from Overseas Citizens Services (Tel from US: 1-888-407-4747 and from overseas: 317-472-2328). You will need to speak to the American Citizens Services unit of the Consular Section. If you are scheduled to leave the foreign country shortly, provide the Consular Section with details regarding your departure schedule.

When you report the loss, theft or misplacement of your passport you must execute an affidavit fully describing the circumstances under which it was lost or stolen. US Department of State form DS-64 can be used for this purpose or you can simply execute a sworn statement before the consular officer describing what happened. A police report is not mandatory but may be required when the embassy/consulate believes a problem may exist such as possible fraud. An applicant eligible to receive a passport should not be placed in circumstances to miss a plane or unreasonably delay travel to obtain a police report. Fuller information is available at http://travel.state.gov/lost_passports_abroadhtml.

Driving licence
In the UK

Here the process depends upon whether you have lost one of the newer 'photocard' driving licences or an older paper licence. Either way you have to deal with the Driver and Vehicle Licensing Agency (DVLA). If you find your licence after receiving a duplicate you should return the original licence to the Agency with an explanatory note.

If you have a photocard and if both parts of your licence, the photocard and the paper counterpart, have been lost or stolen and provided none of the details on your licence have changed or are incorrect you can apply for a duplicate licence using a credit or debit card. To use this service telephone DVLA on 0870 240 0009 between 8.00 am and 8.30 pm Monday to Friday and 8.00 am to 5.30 pm on Saturday.

Alternatively, to make a postal application because one or both parts of your photocard/counterpart has been lost or stolen or there are changes to your details, or if you simply prefer to apply in this way, you will need to complete an application form D1. This is available from most Post Offices. It should be sent, with the photocard/counterpart (if available) and the appropriate fee, to DVLA, Swansea, SA99 1AB.

If you have an old-style paper licence and this has been lost, stolen, destroyed or defaced you must apply for a photocard licence by completing both the D1 application form available from most Post Offices. These should be sent with the appropriate fee, a recent passport-sized colour photograph and the appropriate identity document(s) to DVLA, Swansea, SA99 1AB.

In the US

You should contact your state Department of Motor Vehicles (DMV) to find out what its procedures are. You may be able to put a fraud alert on your license. If the thief has been using your license to commit fraud, or if a new license has been issued to the thief then you may need to change your driver's license number.

Details of state DMVs are available from the American Association of Motor Vehicle Administrators at http://www.aamva.org/links/mnu_linkJurisdictions.asp or by telephone on 703-522-4200.

National Insurance number card

If your NI Number Card is lost or stolen you should report it to your nearest Social Security office (now called JobCentre Plus, part of the Department for Work and Pensions) or Inland Revenue (NI Contributions) office.

You can find your nearest Social Security office online at http://www.jobcentreplus.gov.uk/cms.asp?Page=/Home/AboutUs/OurOffices or by calling 020 7712 2171 (9.00 am—5.00 pm Monday-Friday) or writing to:

Department for Work and Pensions
Correspondence Unit
Room 540, The Adelph
1—11 John Adam Street
London WC2N 6HT

To find your nearest Inland Revenue office see: http://www.inlandrevenue.gov.uk/local/index.htm or tel: 0191 213 5000.

If you want a replacement card you will need to complete an application form. However you are only allowed one replacement throughout your entire life.

Social Security number and card

If your Social Security card has been lost or stolen the Social Security Administration takes no special action, but you should apply for a replacement card by completing Form SS-5, which is available for download from: http://www.socialsecurity.gov/replace_sscard.html, tel: 1-800-772-1213 or visit your local Social Security office. If you think someone is using your number to work, you should contact Social Security. One way to find out whether someone is using your number to work is to check your Social Security Statement. The Statement lists earnings posted to your Social Security record. If you find an error on your Statement, contact Social Security right away.

Restoring your credit rating

One of the worst side-effects of identity theft is damage to your credit rating. The thieves will take out loans and credit cards in your name then default on them, leaving you to take the blame. All of this negative information can end up on your credit report. If the identity thief's actions have damaged your credit rating then you will have to work to put things right and this will take time and effort. The good news is that there are laws and procedures in both the UK and the US to help you do this.

Most agencies advise against using the services of 'credit repair' companies, especially those that require an up-front fee. By enforcing your rights you can achieve everything that they can do, if not everything that they promise.

It can take time for credit information to show up on your file and older records can sometimes be reinstated in error, long after they were deleted. Because of this, the key to properly restoring your credit rating is to check your file regularly, especially before applying for credit.

When you dispute incorrect information in your credit report remember to follow up telephone conversations in writing and keeping proper records.

In the UK

You have a legal right under the Consumer Credit Act 1974 to have incorrect information on your credit file corrected.

If the file contains mistakes, the agency must correct them and tell you what it has done within 28 days. You should inform the agency of any errors within 60 days of receiving your report. If you are not satisfied with the amendment, you can have a notice of correction of up to 200 words added to your file. It will be sent out whenever your credit record is accessed in the future. Free advice is available from your local Citizens' Advice Bureau and from the CRAs themselves.

In the US

The procedures for correcting mistakes on your credit report are set out by the Fair Credit Reporting Act (FCRA). Under the FCRA, both the credit bureau and the information provider, such as a bank or credit card company, are responsible for correcting inaccurate or incomplete information in your report.

When you contact the credit bureau be clear as to which items you are disputing and provide supporting evidence where possible. If you have it include the police report and the Identity Theft Affidavit. Remember, send copies, never originals. You should also write to the information provider with the same information.

The credit bureau's investigation must be completed within 30 days (45 days if you provide additional documents). If the credit bureau does not consider your dispute frivolous (in which case it must tell you so within five business days) it must forward all relevant documents you provide about the dispute to the information provider. The information provider then must investigate and report the results to the credit bureau. If the information provider finds the disputed information to be inaccurate, it must notify any nationwide credit bureau to which it reports, so that the credit bureau can correct this information in your file.

The FTC points out that:

- 🔒 Disputed information that cannot be verified must be deleted from your file;
- 🔒 If your report contains erroneous information, the credit bureau must correct it;
- 🔒 If your file shows an account that belongs to someone else, the credit bureau must delete it;
- 🔒 When the investigation is complete, the credit bureau must give you the written results and, if the dispute results in a change, a free copy of your report;
- 🔒 If an item is changed or removed, the credit bureau cannot put the disputed information back in your file unless the information provider verifies its accuracy and completeness, and the credit bureau gives you a written notice that includes the name, address and phone number of the information provider.

As in the UK, if you are not satisfied with the outcome, you can have a notice of dispute of up to 100 words added to your file. It will be sent out whenever your credit record is accessed in the future.

Clearing your name of the identity thief's crimes

This is the worst-case scenario and the one in which you are most likely to need legal representation. The identity thief commits a crime using your identity and you are held responsible. Often it can be a long time before you find out, discovering the deception only when you are turned down for a job, are sacked, receive a court summons or, worst of all, are arrested.

If you are lucky, the police will have the real criminal's fingerprints and photograph. This can help prove that the criminal wasn't you. If not, they may have his or her signature, in which case expert analysis may be some help.

How to find out if a crime has been committed in your name

In the US, court records are open so querying local, state and federal files by name, date of birth and Social Security number can be a good start. There are also background checking services and private investigators who may be able to identify any judgments or warrants in your name.

In the UK, such records are considered to be private. However, under the Data Protection Act you are entitled to receive a copy of any information held about you. Ask at your local police station to submit a subject access request. This will be forwarded to the National Identification Service, who will reply within 40 days.

Both civil liberties groups and law enforcement agencies are aware of the problem and have advice on how to deal with it. In California the Privacy Rights Clearinghouse and the Identity Theft Resource Center have comprehensive fact sheets available.

In the case of criminal charges, however, my first act would be to find a competent criminal lawyer.

Useful Contacts

Government

UK

UK Passport Service
Tel: 0870 521 0410
http://www.ukpa.gov.uk/_1_applications/1_lost_stolen.asp

Foreign and Commonwealth Office
Tel: 0870 606 0290
www.fco.gov.uk

DVLA
Tel: 0870 240 0009
DVLA, Swansea, SA99 1AB

Department for Work and Pensions
Correspondence Unit
Room 540, The Adelphi
1–11 John Adam Street, London
WC2N 6HT
Tel: 020 7712 2171
http://www.jobcentreplus.gov.uk/cms.asp?Page=/Home/About
Us/OurOffices

Inland Revenue
Tel: 0191 213 5000
http://www.inlandrevenue.gov.uk/local/index.htm

The Home Office Public Enquiry Team
Home Office
7th Floor
50 Queen Anne's Gate
London SW1H 9AT
Tel: 0870 000 1585
Fax: 020 7273 2065
Textphone: 020 7273 3476
public.enquiries@homeoffice.gsi.gov.uk
http://www.homeoffice.gov.uk/crime/fraud/
http://www.identity-theft.org.uk

US
Social Security Administration
Office of Public Inquiries
Windsor Park Building
6401 Security Blvd
Baltimore, MD 21235
Tel: 1-800-772-1213
TTY : 1-800-325-0778
http://www.socialsecurity.gov

Identity Theft Clearinghouse
Federal Trade Commission
600 Pennsylvania Avenue
NW, Washington
DC 20580
Tel: 1-877-IDTHEFT (438-4338)
TDD: 202-326-2502
www.consumer.gov/idtheft

Consumer Response Center
Federal Trade Commission
600 Pennsylvania
NW, H-130, Washington
DC 20580
Tel: 1-877-FTC-HELP (382-4357)

US Department of State Passport Services
Consular Lost/Stolen Passport Section
1111 19th Street
NW, Suite 500, Washington
DC 20036
Tel 202-955-0430
http://travel.state.gov/lost_stolen.html

Overseas Citizen Services
Tel: 1-888-407-4747
Tel from overseas: 317-472-2328
http://travel.state.gov/links.html

American Association of
Motor Vehicle Administrators
Tel: 703-522-4200
http://www.aamva.org/links/mnu_linkJurisdictions.asp

Canada

Key documents issued by the federal government include your Social Insurance Card, Passport, Citizenship and Immigration Documents and the Certificate of Indian Status.

For information on Government of Canada programs and services:
Tel: 1-800-O-Canada (1-800-622-6232)
TTY: 1-800-465-7735
http://www.canada.gc.ca

Replacement ID
http://canada.gc.ca/cdns/wallet/wallet_e.html#app

Office of the Privacy Commissioner
112 Kent Street
Ottawa, ON, K1A 1H3
Tel: 1-800-282-1376
info@privcom.gc.ca
http://www.privcom.gc.ca/fs-fi/02_05_d_10_e.asp

Passport Office
Foreign Affairs Canada
Gatineau, Canada
K1A 0G3
http://www.ppt.gc.ca/passport_office/about_e.asp

Australia
Australian Securities and Investments Commission
Tel: 1 300 300 630
International tel: +61 3 5177 3777
infoline@asic.gov.au
http://www.fido.asic.gov.au/fido/fido.nsf/byheadline/Scams+&+S
windlers+portal?opendocument

Office of the Federal Privacy Commissioner
GPO Box 5218
Sydney NSW 2001
Tel: 1 300 363 992
TTY: 1 800 620 241
Fax: 61 2 9284 9666
privacy@privacy.gov.au
http://www.privacy.gov.au/

Australian Passport Information Service
Tel: 131 232
http://www.passports.gov.au/Web/renewal/lost_stolen.aspx

New Zealand
Privacy Commissioner
PO Box 466
Auckland
Tel: 0800 803 909
Fax: 09 302 2305
privacy@iprolink.co.nz
http://www.cab.org.nz/index.html

New Zealand's Department of Internal Affairs
46 Waring Taylor Street
PO Box 805
Wellington
Tel: 04 495 7200
info@dia.govt.nz or webmaster@dia.govt.nz
http://www.passports.govt.nz/diawebsite.nsf

Law Enforcement

UK
Metropolitan Police Fraud Alert Website
http://www.metpolice.uk/fraudalert/

Association of Chief Police Officers (ACPO)
National Working Group on Fraud
http://www.uk-fraud.info/index.html

Local police
Contact details for your local police force will be in the phone book or can be obtained from
http://www.police.uk/forces/default.asp

Royal Mail
If you believe mail theft is involved you should also report it to the Royal Mail Customer Enquiry Number on 08457 740740.

The Dedicated Cheque and Plastic Crime Unit
Tel: 020 7382 2960
Fax: 020 7382 2999
http://www.dcpcu.org.uk/

US
US Secret Service Field Offices
http://www.secretservice.gov/field_offices.shtml

US Secret Service
Office of Government Liaison and Public Affairs
245 Murray Drive, Building 410
Washington, DC 20223
Tel: 202-406-5708

Federal Bureau of Investigation
935 Pennsylvania Avenue, NW
Room 7350
Washington, DC 20535
Tel: 202-324-3000
http://www.fbi.gov/contact/fo/fo.htm

US Postal Inspection Service
Inspection Service Operations Support Group
Attn: Mail Fraud, Ste 1250
222 S Riverside Plaza
Chicago, IL 60606-6100
http://www.usps.com/ncsc/locators/find-is.html

US Department of Justice
950 Pennsylvania Avenue
NW, Washington
DC 20530-0001
Office of the Attorney General
Tel: 202-353-1555
AskDOJ@usdoj.gov

Canada
RCMP Headquarters
1200 Vanier Parkway
Ottawa, ON
K1A 0R2
Tel: 613-993-7267
TTY: 613-993-3887
http://www.rcmp-grc.gc.ca/scams/identity_e.htm

PhoneBusters The Canadian Antifraud Call Centre
Tel: 1-888-495-8501
Fax: 1-888-654-9426
info@phonebusters.com
www.phonebusters.com

Australia
AFP National Headquarters
68 Northbourne Avenue
Canberra ACT 2601
PO Box 401
Canberra City ACT 2601
Tel: 02 6256 7777
http://www.afp.gov.au/

New Zealand
Office of the Commissioner
PO Box 3017
Wellington
Tel: +64 4 474-9499
Fax: +64 4 498-7400
http://www.police.govt.nz/contact.php
http://www.ns.org.nz/15.html

Banking
UK
Banking Code Standards Board
33 St James's Square
London SW1Y 4JS
Tel: 0845 230 9694
Fax: 020 7661 9784
helpline@bcsb.org.uk
http://www.bankingcode.org.uk/home.htm

Association for Payment Clearing Services
Mercury House
Triton Court
14 Finsbury Square
London EC2A 1LQ
Tel: 020 7711 6200
Fax: 020 7256 5527
http://www.apacs.org.uk

Card Watch c/o APACS
Tel: 020 7711 6356
Fax: 020 7628 0927
cardwatch@apacs.org.uk
http://www.cardwatch.org.uk/

US
American Bankers Association
1120 Connecticut Avenue
NW, Washington
DC 20036
Tel: 1-800-BANKERS (226-5377)
http://www.aba.com/default.htm

National Credit Union Administration
1775 Duke Street
Alexandria, VA 22314-3428
Tel: 703-518-6300
http://www.ncua.gov/

Canada
Ombudsman for Banking Services and Investments
PO Box 896
Station Adelaide
Toronto, ON
M5C 2K3
Tel: 1-888-451-4519
Fax: 1-888-422-2865
Toronto area tel: 416-287-2877
Toronto area fax: 416-225-4722
ombudsman@obsi.ca
http://www.obsi.ca/obsi/pages_english/ehome.php3

Canadian Bankers Association
Box 348
Commerce Court West
199 Bay Street, 30th Floor
Toronto, ON
M5L 1G2
Tel.: 416-362-6092
Fax: 416-362-770
http://www.cba.ca/en/consumer.asp

Australia
Australian Bankers' Association
Level 3
56 Pitt Street
Sydney NSW 2000
Tel: +61 2 8298 0417

Fax: +61 2 8298 0402
reception@bankers.asn.au
http://www.bankers.asn.au/

Banking and Financial Services Ombudsman
GPO Box 3
Melbourne VIC 3001
Tel: 1 300 78 08 08 (Monday to Friday, 9 am to 5 pm
AEST)
Fax: 03 9613 7345

New Zealand
Banking Ombudsman
P O Box 10-573
Wellington
Tel: 0800 805 950
Fax: 04 471 0548
help@bankombudsman.org.nz
www.bankombudsman.org.nz

New Zealand Bankers' Association
Level 12, Grand Arcade Building
16 Willis Street, PO Box 3043
Wellington
Tel: 04 472 8838
Fax: 04 473 1698
nzba@nzba.org.nz
http://www.nzba.org.nz/public.htm

Credit Reference/Reporting Agencies

UK

Experian Ltd
Consumer Help Service,
PO Box 9000,
Nottingham NG80 7WP
Tel: 0870 241 6212
www.experian.co.uk

Equifax plc
Credit File Advice Centre
PO Box 1140
Bradford BD1 5US
Tel: 08705 143700
www.equifax.co.uk

Callcredit plc
Consumer Services Team
PO Box 491
Leeds LS3 1WZ
Tel: 0870 060 1414
www.callcredit.plc.uk

CIFAS
4th Floor, Central House
14 Upper Woburn Place
London WC1H 0NN
http://www.cifas.org.uk

For CIFAS protective registration you can phone Equifax on 0870 010 2091, email protective.registrationuk@equifax.com, or download the form from http://www.cifas.org.uk/protreg.htm

US
Equifax
For obtaining your credit report by mail, phone or online:
PO Box 740241
Atlanta, GA 30374-0241
Tel: 800-685-1111
www.equifax.com

Hearing impaired call: 1-800-255-0056 and ask the operator to call the Auto Disclosure Line at 1-800-685-1111 to request a copy of your report.

To report fraud, call and write to:
PO Box 740241
Atlanta, GA 30374-0241
Tel: 800-525-6285

Experian
For obtaining your credit report by mail, phone or online:
PO Box 2002, Allen TX 75013
Tel: 888-EXPERIAN (397-3742)
www.experian.com

To report fraud, call and write:
PO Box 9530, Allen TX 75013
Tel: 888-EXPERIAN (397-3742)
TDD: 1-800-972-0322

Trans Union
For obtaining your credit report by mail, phone or online:
PO Box 1000
Chester, PA 19022
Tel: 800-888-4213
www.transunion.com

To report fraud, call and write to:
Fraud Victim Assistance Division,
PO Box 6790, Fullerton, CA 92634
Tel: 800-680-7289
TDD: 1-877-553-7803

Check verification companies:
TeleCheck
Tel: 1-800-710-9898 or 927-0188

Certegy Inc
Tel: 1-800-437-5120

International Check Services
Tel: 1-800-631-9656
Call SCAN (1-800-262-7771) to find out if the identity
thief has been passing bad cheques in your name.

Canadian
Equifax Canada Inc
Consumer Relations Department
Box 190 Jean Talon Station
Montreal, Quebec, H1S 2Z2
Tel: 1-800-465-7166/514- 493-2314
consumer.relations@equifax.com
http://www.equifax.com/EFX_Canada/

TransUnion Canada
http://www.tuscores.ca/Personal/index.jsp?locale=en_CA
Tel: 1-877-525-3823
Fraud Victim Assistance Department: 905-525-9986
For residents of all provinces except Quebec:
Consumer Relations Centre
PO Box 338, LCD 1
Hamilton, ON L8L 7W2

Tel: 1-866-525-0262 or 905-525-0262 (Monday to Friday, 8 am to 8 pm EST)
For residents of Quebec:
1600 Henri Bourassa Boul Ouest, Suite 210
Montreal, PQ
H3M 3E2
Tel: 1-877-713-3393 or 514-335-0374 (Monday to Thursday, 8.30 am to 5 pm EST, Friday 8.30 am to 4.30 pm EST)

Australia
Baycorp Advantage
PO Box 964
North Sydney NSW 2059
Tel: 02 9464 6000
http://www.mycreditfile.com.au/

Dun & Bradstreet (Australia) Pty Ltd
Public Access Centre, PO Box 7405
St Kilda Road VIC 3004
http://www.dnb.com.au
https://secure.dnb.com.au/ccb/AU/your_credit_file.asp

New Zealand
Dun & Bradstreet (New Zealand) Pty Ltd
Public Access Centre
PO Box 9589 Newmarket
Auckland 1031
https://secure.dnb.com.au/ccb/NZ/your_credit_file.asp

Baycorp Advantage
PO Box 90845
Victoria Street
Auckland
Tel: 09 356 5800
Fax: 09 356 5849

assistnz@baycorpadvantage.com http://www.baycorpadvan-tage.com/personal_information/my_credit_file.asp

Non-profit organisations

UK
Your Rights (Liberty's online guide to human rights law for England and Wales)
http://www.yourrights.org.uk/index.shtml

US
Privacy Rights Clearinghouse
3100 5th Ave, Suite B
San Diego, CA 92103
Tel: 619-298-3396
Fax: 619-298-5681
http://www.privacyrights.org/

Identity Theft Resource Center
PO Box 26833
San Diego CA 92196
San Diego, California
Tel: 858-693-7935 (PST)
itrc@idtheftcenter.org
www.idtheftcenter.org

Phantom Withdrawals (online resources for victims of ATM fraud)
http://www.cl.cam.ac.uk/~mkb23/phantom/

The Anti-Phishing Working Group (APWG)
info@antiphishing.org
http://www.antiphishing.org/

Electronic Privacy Information Center
1718 Connecticut Ave. NW
Suite 200, Washington
DC 20009
http://www.epic.org/

Canada
Office of Consumer Affairs
235 Queen Street
Ottawa, ON
K1A 0H5
Tel: 613-957-8717
Fax: 613-952-6927
info@cmcweb.ca
http://cmcweb.ic.gc.ca/epic/internet/incmc-
cmc.nsf/en/fe00040e.html

Australia
Office of Consumer and Business Affairs
GPO Box 1719
Adelaide SA 5001
Tel: 08 8204 9777
South Australian tel: 131 882
Fax: 08 8204 9769
www.ocba.sa.gov.au

New Zealand
Citizen Advise Bureaux
Tel: 0800 367 222
http://www.cab.org.nz

About the Author

Robert Hamadi was born in Jarrow, northeast England and studied engineering at Cambridge University. As Head of Communications at The Publishers Association he leads on high technology crime issues and liaison with law enforcement, and has worked on cases from the UK to the former Soviet Union. He is the founding chair of the Digital Content Forum's Cybercrime Industry Action Group, attends the Home Office/National High Technology Crime Unit Internet Crime Forum on behalf of the Internet Enforcement Group of the British Content Industries and is a member of the Rating and Filtering Sub-group of the Home Secretary's Taskforce on Child Protection on the Internet. In 2002 he led a fact-finding mission to the USA for the Department of Trade and Industry. As a result of the mission team's in-depth consultation with Federal Law Enforcement agencies a broad cross-section of the UK content industries began work on a new regime for policing copyright issues on the internet. From 1998 to 2002 he served as a London borough councillor.